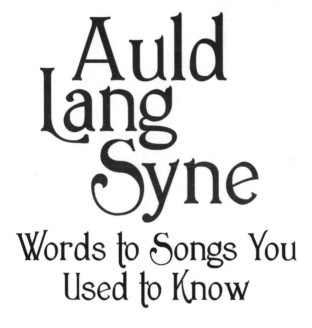

Auld Lang Syne

Words to Songs You Used to Know

Compiled by
Karen Dolby

Michael O'Mara Books Limited

First published in Great Britain in 2015 by
Michael O'Mara Books Limited
9 Lion Yard
Tremadoc Road
London SW4 7NQ

A CIP catalogue record for this book is available from the British Library.

Papers used by Michael O'Mara Books Limited are natural, recyclable products
made from wood grown in sustainable forests. The manufacturing processes
conform to the environmental regulations of the country of origin.

ISBN: 978-1-78243-426-9 in hardback print format
ISBN: 978-1-78243-543-3 in e-book format

1 2 3 4 5 6 7 8 9 10

www.mombooks.com

Cover design by Ana Bjezancevic
Designed and typeset by Tetragon, London

Printed and bound by CPI Group (UK) Ltd, Croydon, CR0 4YY

Auld
Lang
Syne

Contents

CONTENTS

Introduction

Everyone has their own personal soundtrack running throughout their life, with certain songs that can instantly transport you back to 'that' summer, a teenage holiday, or particular place or time. Music and memories intertwine and it is not only modern music that resonates; older tunes also linger, and snatches of half-forgotten lyrics can spring to mind although we often have no idea when we first heard them.

Songs have been sung in every area of life: by factory workers, sailors, soldiers, mothers and grandparents; they were sung on journeys, in fields, music halls and pleasure gardens, and at country fairs. Many told of love, both happy and sad, relationships, everyday work and life's concerns. They were as likely to come from the workhouse as the parish church, the schoolyard as the local tavern. Sometimes words and melodies were composed together but tunes were also 'borrowed' from older existing songs. They were learned by rote and rarely written down. Traditionally, songs were passed on from generation to generation, through impromptu performances within families and at social gatherings. In the pre-technology days, when people 'made their own entertainment', they were sung whenever and wherever people got together. They are essentially everyday music from a time when the only music heard was live.

Popular songs took on a life of their own as they travelled across countries and oceans; along the way different singers would add their own embellishments to make the words their own. Variations developed over the years and there are often several versions of the same song as they have been adapted to suit the singer or a specific place or event. In this book I have tried to choose the most authentic, or best-known lyrics, but everyone will have their favourite version and so I apologize if it is not the one included here.

Coming from a largely oral tradition it can be difficult to find records of very old lyrics. Plays, memoirs and novels can be good sources for references to the songs of the day, and from the eighteenth century cheaply produced broadsides and street literature printed words and music. In addition, many Christmas songs and carols were originally noted down with illustrations in chapbooks, which were circulated particularly in London and other cities.

The oral tradition received a boost in the nineteenth century when a growing interest in vernacular music and the songs of the people inspired individuals to record and publish them for the first time. In Britain, there were various collectors, including the Reverend Sabine Baring-Gould and Frank Kidson, who would travel the country gathering together songs from local people. Often, such collectors were inspired by Thomas Percy's work a century earlier following his discovery of a manuscript of ancient ballads. Towards the end of the century Cecil Sharp, Ralph Vaughan Williams and Percy Grainger began their work and the Folk-Song Society was formed in England in 1898. In the US, individuals such as Alan Lomax (who was followed into the field by his son) were also making their mark, founding societies, publishing collections and organizing field studies. In Australia and

Canada, contributions were also being made by musicologists and collectors such as Clive Carey and, later, Edith Fowke. Collectors noted down words and music and, just as performers had, they introduced their own variations, sometimes cleaning up lyrics considered too bawdy for respectable ears.

Traditional songs remained popular and continued to develop, with new lyrics and melodies adding to the canon. However, as the twentieth century progressed singing within communities declined with the ready availability of recorded music of all types. There was something of a folk revival in the late fifties and early sixties when a new wave of folk singers began recording the old songs to vinyl, but by the end of the decade the emphasis had shifted towards contemporary, non-traditional folk music.

Some songs are short and simple, but many spin an enticing yarn and pack a great deal of emotion into their verses. There's humour and irony, pathos, regret, love and sorrow. They tell of faraway places and the minutiae of home, offering a glimpse of other lives and times. They are a great social catalogue.

It is surprising just how many old songs have slipped into popular culture, not only through modern recordings and interpretations, but also through films, adverts and television. A few notes of a half-remembered tune can bring a stadium to its feet, crooning along, or conjure memories of schooldays or bedtime lullabies. Good songs stick and simply refuse to be forgotten, or rather not completely. Often we know the chorus or a few lines, the rest remaining tantalizingly out of reach. This book aims to provide the missing verses, along the way celebrating the wonderful diversity of songs, shanties, ballads and anthems that wind through our collective history and bind us together.

CHAPTER 1

Parsley, Sage, Rosemary & Thyme: Country Life

The countryside and rural life were particularly popular themes with Victorian song collectors, who travelled the country to record lyrics and research local traditions, although some of the songs actually originated in towns where idealized pictures of a pastoral idyll appealed to industrial communities. This interest in folk songs from a bygone era, never before written down, continued into the twentieth century, throughout the British Isles and North America.

❧ SCARBOROUGH FAIR ❧

Are you going to Scarborough Fair?
Parsley, sage, rosemary and thyme.
Remember me to one who lives there,
She once was a true love of mine.

Have her to make me a cambric shirt,
Parsley, sage, rosemary and thyme.
Without no seams, nor fine needle work,
Then she'll be a true love of mine.

Tell her to weave it in a sycamore wood lane,
Parsley, sage, rosemary and thyme.
Gather it up in a basket of flowers,
Then she'll be a true love of mine.

Have her wash it in yonder dry well,
Parsley, sage, rosemary and thyme.
Where water ne'er sprung, nor drop of rain fell,
Then she'll be a true love of mine.

Tell her to find me an acre of land,
Parsley, sage, rosemary and thyme.
Between the sea foam and over the sand,
Then she'll be a true love of mine.

Plow the land with the horn of a lamb,
Parsley, sage, rosemary and thyme.
Then sow some seeds from north of the dam,
Then she'll be a true love of mine.

Have her reap it with a sickle of leather,
Parsley, sage, rosemary and thyme.
Gather it up in a bunch of heather,
Then she'll be a true love of mine.

If she tells me she can't, then I'll reply,
Parsley, sage, rosemary and thyme.
Let me know, that at least she will try,
Then she'll be a true love of mine.

Love imposes impossible tasks,
Parsley, sage, rosemary and thyme.
Though not more than any heart asks,
And I must know she's a true love of mine.

When thou has finished thy task,
Parsley, sage, rosemary and thyme.
Come to me my hand for to ask,
For then you'll be a true love of mine.

Parsley for comfort, sage for strength, rosemary love and thyme courage. These herbs could be the ingredients of a medieval love charm, or the line may be nothing more than a romantic-sounding nineteenth-century addition. The fair in Scarborough was an annual event, lasting some weeks, and dated back to the thirteenth century, but it is not clear exactly how old this well-known folk song really is. Some versions refer to other towns or fairs, and the lyrics possibly have their roots in an older Celtic or Scottish song called 'The Elfin Knight'. The wording varies but always includes impossible tasks set as a riddle for a man's former lover, to prove her true love.

❧ COUNTRY GARDENS ❧

How many gentle flowers grow
In an English country garden?
I'll tell you now of some that I know,
And those I miss I hope you'll pardon.
Daffodils, hearts-ease and flox,
Meadow sweet and lilies, stocks,
Gentle lupins and tall hollyhocks,
Roses, fox-gloves, snowdrops, forget-me-nots,
In an English country garden.

How many insects find their home
In an English country garden?
I'll tell you now of some that I know,
And those I miss I hope you'll pardon.
Dragonflies, moths and bees,
Spiders falling from the trees,
Butterflies sway in the mild gentle breeze.
There are hedgehogs that roam,
And little garden gnomes,
In an English country garden.

How many song-birds make their nest
In an English country garden?
I'll tell you now of some that I know,
And those I miss I hope you'll pardon.
Babbling, coo-cooing doves,

Robins and the warbling thrush,
Blue birds, lark, finch and nightingale.
We all smile in the spring,
When the birds all start to sing,
In an English country garden.

Today more famously known as 'English Country Garden' –
released by Jimmie Rodgers in 1962 it reached number five
in the UK singles charts – 'Country Gardens' was originally
a Morris dancers' tune and was among the songs collected
by Cecil Sharp. It was then arranged for the piano by Percy
Grainger in 1918. The song became a favourite with school
orchestras and there are many popular recordings along with
some parodies of the lyrics.

STRAWBERRY FAIR

As I was going to Strawberry Fair,
Singing, singing, buttercups and daisies,
I met a maiden taking her ware,
Fol-de-dee!
Her eyes were blue and golden her hair,
As she went on to Strawberry Fair.
Ri-fol, ri-fol, tol-de-riddle-li-do,
Ri-fol, ri-fol, tol-de-riddle-dee.

'Kind sir, pray pick of my basket!' she said,
Singing, singing, buttercups and daisies,
'My cherries ripe, or my roses red,
Fol-de-dee!
My strawberries sweet, I can of them spare,
As I go on to Strawberry Fair.'
Ri-fol, ri-fol, tol-de-riddle-li-do,
Ri-fol, ri-fol, tol-de-riddle-dee.

Your cherries soon will be wasted away,
Singing, singing, buttercups and daisies,
Your roses wither and never stay,
Fol-de-dee!
'Tis not to seek such perishing ware,
That I am tramping to Strawberry Fair.
Ri-fol, ri-fol, tol-de-riddle-li-do,
Ri-fol, ri-fol, tol-de-riddle-dee.

I want to purchase a generous heart,
Singing, singing, buttercups and daisies,
A tongue that is neither nimble nor tart,
Tol-de-dee!
An honest mind, but such trifles are rare,
I doubt if they're found at Strawberry Fair.
Ri-fol, ri-fol, tol-de-riddle-li-do,
Ri-fol, ri-fol, tol-de-riddle-dee.

The price I offer, my sweet pretty maid,
Singing, singing, buttercups and daisies,
A ring of gold on your finger displayed,
Tol-de-dee!

So come, make over to me your ware
In church today at Strawberry Fair.
Ri-fol, ri-fol, tol-de-riddle-li-do,
Ri-fol, ri-fol, tol-de-riddle-dee.

The words and melody were first recorded in Devon in 1891 by the English musical editor and cleric Henry Fleetwood Sheppard, and the song was widely known throughout Devon and Cornwall at that time. The original, more bawdy, lyrics were probably sanitized by Sheppard's collaborator, the Reverend Sabine Baring-Gould.

THE HAWTHORN TREE

It was a maid of my country
As she came by a hawthorn tree,
As full of flow'rs as might be seen
She marvel'd to see the tree so green.

At last she asked of this tree,
How came this freshness unto thee,
And ev'ry branch so fair and clean?
I marvel that you grow so green.

The tree made answer by and by,
I have cause to grow triumphantly,
The sweetest dew that ever be seen
Doth fall on me to keep me green.

Yea, quoth the maid, but where you grow
You stand at hand for ev'ry bow,
Of ev'ry man for to be seen,
I marvel that you grow so green.

Though many one take flow'rs from me,
And many a branch out of my tree,
I have such store they will not be seen
For more and more my twigs grow green.

But how, an' they chance to cut thee down,
And carry thy branches into the town?
Then they will never more be seen
To grow again so fresh and green.

Though that you do it is no boot,
Altho' they cut me to the root,
Next year again I will be seen
To bud my branches fresh and green.

And you, fair maid, cannot do so,
For when your beauty once does go
Then will it never more be seen,
As I with my branches can grow green.

The maid with that began to blush
And turn'd her from the hawthorn bush
She thought herself so fair and clean,
Her beauty still would ever grow green.

> But after this never could I hear
> Of this fair maiden anywhere,
> That ever she was in forest seen
> To talk again with the hawthorn green.

Printed in William Chappell's collection *Popular Music of the Olden Time* (1810), where it was described as an 'ancient' song, 'The Hawthorn Tree' also appears in John Playford's dancing manual of 1651, *The English Dancing Master*. There, it was called 'Dargeson' or 'The Sedany', which was a country dance. Dargeson may be a place name or refer to an old children's piece that was performed at the Blackfriars Theatre in 1606 by the troupe of child actors known as the Children of the Revels.

ON ILKLA MOOR BAHT 'AT

Whear 'as tha' been sin' ah saw thee, ah saw thee?
On Ilkla Moor baht 'at,
Whear 'as tha' been sin' ah saw thee?
Whear 'as tha' been sin' ah saw thee?

CHORUS:
> *On Ilkla Moor baht 'at,*
> *On Ilkla Moor baht 'at,*
> *On Ilkla Moor baht 'at.*

Tha's been a-courtin' Mary Jayun, Mary Jayun,
On Ilkla Moor baht 'at,

Tha's been a-courtin' Mary, tha's been a-courtin' Mary,
Tha's been a-courtin' Mary Jayun.

CHORUS

Tha'll go an' get thee death o'cowld, death o'cowld,
On Ilkla Moor baht 'at,
Tha'll go an' get thee death o', tha'll go an' get thee death o',
Tha'll go an' get thee death o'cowld.

CHORUS

Then we shall ha' to bury thee, bury thee,
On Ilkla Moor baht 'at,
Then we shall ha' to bury, then we shall ha' to bury,
Then we shall ha' to bury thee.

CHORUS

Then t'worms'll cum an' et thee oop, et thee oop,
On Ilkla Moor baht 'at,
Then t'worms'll cum an' et thee, then t'worms'll cum an'
    et thee,
Then t'worms'll cum an' et thee oop.

CHORUS

Then t'doox'll cum an' et oop t'worms, et oop t'worms,
On Ilkla Moor baht 'at,
Then t'doox'll cum an' et oop, then t'doox'll cum an' et
    oop,
Then t'doox'll cum an' et oop t'worms.

CHORUS

Then us'll cum an' et oop t'doox, et oop t'doox,
On Ilkla Moor baht 'at,

Then us'll cum an' et oop, then us'll cum an' et oop,
Then us'll cum an' et oop t'doox.

CHORUS

Then us'll all 'av etten thee, etten thee,
On Ilkla Moor baht 'at,
Then us'll all 'av etten, then us'll all 'av etten,
Then us'll all 'av etten thee.

CHORUS

That's whear we'll get our owen back, owen back,
On Ilkla Moor baht 'at,
That's whear we'll get our owen, that's whear we'll get
    our owen,
That's whear we'll get our owen back.

CHORUS

Sung in a Yorkshire dialect, the song tells of a foolish young man out on Ilkley Moor without a hat in pursuit of his sweetheart, Mary Jane. The tale ends with the singers teaching the poor hatless man a lesson, having eaten the ducks (t'doox), that had eaten the worms, that had feasted on the man's buried remains. First published in 1916, the lyrics were probably composed around the middle of the nineteenth century, supposedly by members of Halifax Church choir out on the moor for a picnic and ramble. It was set to the older Methodist hymn tune 'Cranbrook' by Thomas Clark, which is also one of the tunes for 'While Shepherds Watched Their Flocks'.

THE HUNGRY FOX

A hungry fox jumped up in a fright,
And he begged for the moon to give him light,
For he had many miles to trot that night,
Before he got back to his den O, den O, den O,
For he had many miles to trot that night,
Before he got back to his den O.

So he cocked up his head and out went his tail,
And off he went on the long, long trail,
Which he'd done many times in calm and gale,
But he always got back to his den O, den O, den O,
Which he'd done many times in calm and gale,
But he always got back to his den O, den O, den O.

And soon he came to the old farmyard,
Where the ducks and the geese to him were barred,
But he always got one by working hard,
To take back to his den O, den O, den O,
But he always got one by working hard,
To take back to his den O, den O, den O.

He grabbed the grey goose by the neck,
And he slung him right across his back,
And the old grey goose went quack, quack, quack,
But the fox was off to his den O, den O, den O,
And the old grey goose went quack, quack, quack,
But the fox was off to his den O, den O, den O.

Old Mother Slipper Slopper jumped out of bed,
And out of the window she poked her head,
'Oh, John, John, the grey goose is gone,
And the fox is off to his den O, den O, den O,
Oh, John, John, the grey goose is gone,
And the fox is off to his den O, den O, den O.'

John went up to the top of the hill,
And he blew a trumpet loud and shrill,
Said the fox, 'That's very pretty music, still,
I'd rather be in my den O, den O, den O,'
Said the fox, 'That's very pretty music, still,
I'd rather be in my den O, den O, den O.'

At last he got back to his den,
To his dear little foxes eight, nine, ten,
And they've had many fat geese since then,
And sometimes a good fat hen O, hen O, hen O,
And they've had many fat geese since then,
And sometimes a good fat hen O, hen O, hen O.

The earliest versions of this traditional folk song have a long history and a fifteenth-century manuscript in the British Museum shows it written in Middle English. It used to be widely known throughout Britain and North America. Sir Walter Scott included it among his favourites from childhood and it regularly appeared in many Victorian broadsides. Sometimes the fox is called 'Daddy' or 'Father Fox'.

❧ HOME ON THE RANGE ❧

Oh, give me a home where the buffalo roam,
Where the deer and the antelope play,
Where seldom is heard, a discouraging word,
And the skies are not cloudy all day.

CHORUS:
Home, home on the range,
Where the deer and the antelope play;
Where seldom is heard a discouraging word,
And the skies are not cloudy all day.

Where the air is so pure, the zephyrs so free,
The breezes so balmy and light,
That I would not exchange, my home on the range,
For all of the cities so bright.

CHORUS

The red man was pressed from this part of the West,
He's likely no more to return,
To the banks of Red River, where seldom if ever,
Their flickering campfires burn.

CHORUS

How often at night when the heavens are bright,
With the light from the glittering stars,
Have I stood here amazed and asked as I gazed,
If their glory exceeds that of ours.

CHORUS

Oh, I love the wild flowers in this bright land of ours,
I love the wild curlew's shrill scream,
The bluffs and white rocks, and the antelope flocks,
That graze on the mountain tops green.

CHORUS

Oh, give me a land where the bright diamond sand,
Flows leisurely down the stream;
Where the graceful white swan, goes gliding along,
Like a maid in a heavenly dream.

CHORUS

Dr Brewster M. Higley of Smith County, Kansas, wrote the original lyrics as a poem called 'My Western Home' in praise of his new prairie home where he had moved in 1871. It was set to music by his friend Daniel E. Kelley and soon came to be regarded as a classic Western song. The verses have been somewhat changed since their publication as sheet music in 1925 but the song has proved so popular that it was adopted as the official state song of Kansas in 1947.

THE OLD GREY GOOSE

Go tell Aunt Nancy,
Go tell Aunt Nancy,
Go tell Aunt Nancy,
The old grey goose is dead.

The one she's been savin',
The one she's been savin',
The one she's been savin',
To make a feather bed.

She died last Sunday,
She died last Sunday,
She died last Sunday,
Behind the garden shed.

The goslin' are cryin',
The goslin' are cryin',
The goslin' are cryin',
Because their mammy's dead.

Go tell Aunt Nancy,
Go tell Aunt Nancy,
Go tell Aunt Nancy,
The old grey goose is dead.

The name of the aunt varies, and Rhody, Tabby and Sarah are all popularly used. Often sung as a lullaby by pioneer settlers throughout America, this simple song may have originated back across the Atlantic in Ireland. There are alternate verses and sometimes they mention a preacher who tries unsuccessfully to kill the goose for his Sunday dinner.

CHAPTER 2

The Pipes are Calling: Thoughts of Home

These songs date from an era when many were seeking to escape poverty and find their fortune in far-flung countries, and when British men, women and children could find themselves transported thousands of miles to Australia as punishment for the theft of a loaf of bread. Family and friends were often left behind, never to be seen again, and it is not surprising that sentimentality about the homeland and lost loves crept into song lyrics. War and rebellion also separated communities, and the longing of the soldier for home is also reflected. Patriotism, too, is another strong theme.

❦ LOCH LOMOND ❧

By yon bonnie banks and by yon bonnie braes,
Where the sun shines bright on Loch Lomond
Me and my true love were ever wont to gae,
On the bonnie, bonnie banks of Loch Lomond.

CHORUS:
> *O ye'll take the high road and I'll take the low road,*
> *And I'll be in Scotland afore ye,*
> *But me and my true love will never meet again,*
> *On the bonnie, bonnie banks of Loch Lomond.*

'Twas there that we parted in yon shady glen,
On the steep, steep side of Ben Lomond.
Where in the purple hue, the hieland hills we view,
And the moon coming out in the gloaming.

CHORUS

The wee birdies sing and the wild flowers spring,
And in sunshine the waters are sleeping:
But the broken heart it kens, nae second spring again,
Though the waeful may cease frae their greeting.

CHORUS

The lyrics reportedly draw on a Celtic myth that tells of how the soul of a Scot who dies far from home will find its way back by the low road of death. One of many theories surrounding its origin is that the song was written after the Jacobite uprising of 1745. It is said to be about two prisoners held in Carlisle jail: one condemned to death for his support of Bonnie Prince Charlie, and who would be taking the spiritual low road home; the other set free. 'Loch Lomond' was first published in 1841 and the tune is based on an older Scottish air (air meaning a variation on a song).

DANNY BOY

Oh Danny boy, the pipes, the pipes are calling,
From glen to glen, and down the mountain side,
The summer's gone, and all the roses falling,
'Tis you, 'tis you, must go and I must bide.

But come ye back when summer's in the meadow,
Or when the valley's hushed and white with snow,
'Tis I'll be here in sunshine or in shadow,
Oh Danny boy, oh Danny boy, I love you so.

But when you come, when all the flowers are dying,
If I am dead, as dead I well may be,
You'll come and find the place where I am lying,
And kneel and say an 'Ave' there for me.

And I shall hear, tho' soft you tread above me,
And all my grave will warmer, sweeter be,
For you shall bend and tell me that you love me,
And I will sleep in peace until you come to me.

Oh Danny boy, oh Danny boy, I love you so.

The words were written by the English lawyer and lyricist Frederic Weatherly in 1910. He then edited them to fit the tune of 'Londonderry Air' after his Irish-born sister-in-law sent him a copy from the US, and the song was published in 1913. It is sometimes said to be a parent's message to a son about to emigrate to the New World or leaving for war.

FAR AWAY IN AUSTRALIA

Sweetheart I'm bidding you fond farewell,
I will be yours someday,
I'm bound for a new land, my fortune to try,
And I'm ready to sail away.

CHORUS:
Far away in Australia,
Soon will fate be kind,
And I will be ready to welcome at last,
The girl I left behind.

'Oh, you can't leave me,' this poor maid said,
'I will not let you go.'
'But I must leave you,' he gently replied,
'If only for a while, you know.'

'Now in success or in failure,
I will always be true,
And proudly each day in the land far away,
I'll be building a home for you.'

Daily she waits at the old cottage gate,
Watching the whole day through,
Then one day a message from over the sea,
And I'm hoping these words are true.

CHORUS:
Far away in Australia,
Now has come the time,
When I am ready to welcome at last,
The girl I left behind.

After the famine of the 1840s there was a constant stream of impoverished migrants leaving Ireland for a new life. Known as the Irish diaspora, many sailed for America or Australia as 'lands of opportunity', leaving family and lovers behind. It has been estimated that 80 million people worldwide can claim Irish descent.

❧ THE WIND THAT ☙
SHAKES THE BARLEY

I sat within a valley green,
I sat there with my true love,
My sad heart strove the two between,
The old love and the new love.
The old for her, the new that made
Me think of Ireland dearly,
While soft the wind blew down the glade
And shook the golden barley.

'Twas hard the woeful words to frame,
To break the ties that bound us,
'Twas harder still to bear the shame
Of foreign chains around us.
And so I said, 'The mountain glen
I'll seek next morning early,
And join the brave United Men,'
While soft winds shook the barley.

While sad I kissed away her tears,
My fond arms 'round her flinging,
The foeman's shot burst on our ears
From out the wildwood ringing.
A bullet pierced my true love's side,
In life's young spring so early,
And on my breast in blood she died
While soft winds shook the barley.

I bore her to the wildwood screen,
And many a summer blossom,
I placed with branches thick and green
Above her gore-stained bosom.
I wept and kissed her pale, pale cheek,
Then rushed o'er vale and far lea,
My vengeance on the foe to wreak
While soft winds shook the barley.

But blood for blood without remorse,
I've ta'en at Oulart Hollow,
And placed my true love's clay-cold corpse
Where I full soon will follow.
And round her grave I wander drear,
Noon, night and morning early,
With breaking heart whene'er I hear,
The wind that shakes the barley.

The nineteenth-century, Limerick-born poet Robert Dwyer Joyce wrote this Irish rebellion song in 1861. Rebels of the 1798 uprising often carried barley to eat on the march. After battles, the rebels' bodies would be piled in mass graves, where the grains would sprout and mark the spot.

❧ THE OAK ❧
AND THE ASH

A North Country maid up to London had strayed,
Although with her nature it did not agree,
Which made her repent, and so bitterly lament,
Oh, I wish once again for the North Country.

CHORUS:
Oh the oak and the ash and the bonnie ivy tree,
They flourish at home in my own country.

O fain would I be in the North Country,
Where the lads and lasses are making of hay;
There should I see what is pleasant to me,
A mischief light on them entic'd me away!

CHORUS

I like not the court, nor the city resort,
Since there is no fancy for such maids as me;
Their pomp and their pride I can never abide,
Because with my humour it does not agree.

CHORUS

How oft have I been in the Westmoreland green,
Where the young men and maidens resort for to play,
Where we with delight, from morning till night,
Could feast and frolic on each holiday.

CHORUS

The ewes and their lambs, with the kids and their dams,
To see in the country how finely they play;
The bells they do ring, and the birds they do sing,
And the fields and the gardens are pleasant and gay.

CHORUS

At wakes and at fairs, being freed of all cares,
We there with our lovers did use for to dance;
Then hard hap had I, my ill fortune to try,
And so up to London, my steps to advance.

CHORUS

But still I perceive, I a husband might have,
If I to the city my mind could but frame;
But I'll have a lad that is North Country bred,
Or else I'll not marry, in the mind that I am.

CHORUS

A maiden I am, and a maid I'll remain,
Until my own country again I do see,
For here in this place I shall ne'er see the face
Of him that's allotted my love for to be.

CHORUS

Then farewell my daddy, and farewell my mammy,
Until I do see you, I nothing but mourn;
Rememb'ring my brothers, my sisters, and others,
In less than a year I hope to return.

CHORUS

This traditional song has a familiar theme of a country girl seeking fortune and excitement in the capital city, only to find she dislikes it and longs for home. The tune was originally a dance and appeared in James Hawkins' musical transcripts of 1650. The song itself was included in the seventeenth-century Roxburgh collection of ballads where it was called, 'The Northern Lasse's Lamentation' or 'Unhappy Maid's Misfortune'.

I'LL TAKE YOU
HOME AGAIN, KATHLEEN

I'll take you home again, Kathleen,
Across the ocean wild and wide,
To where your heart has ever been,
Since first you were my bonny bride.
The roses all have left your cheeks,
I watched them fade away and die,
Your voice is sad whene'er you speak,
And tears bedim your loving eyes.
So I will take you back Kathleen,
To where your heart will feel no pain,
And when the fields are fresh and green,
I will take you to your home again.

I know you love me Kathleen dear,
Your heart was ever fond and true,
I always feel when you are near,
That life holds nothing dear but you.

The smiles that once you gave to me,
I scarcely ever see them now,
The many, many times I see,
A darkening shadow on your brow.
Oh, so I will take you back Kathleen,
To where your heart will feel no pain,
And when the fields are fresh and green,
I will take you to your home again.

To that dear home beyond the sea,
My Kathleen shall again return,
And when thy old friends welcome thee,
Thy loving heart will cease to yearn.
Where laughs the little silver stream,
Beside your mother's humble cot,
And brightest rays of sunshine gleam,
To where your grief will be forgot.
So, I will take you back Kathleen,
To where your heart will feel no pain,
And when the fields are fresh and green,
I will take you to your home again.

This popular Irish ballad was actually written by an American of German descent in 1875. Thomas Paine Westendorf wrote the song for his wife Jenny in answer to 'Barney, Take Me Home Again', another popular song of the day written by his friend George W. Brown, who sometimes wrote under the name George W. Persley.

❧ DIXIE ❧

Oh, I wish I was in the land of cotton,
Old times there are not forgotten.
Look away, look away, look away, Dixie Land!

In Dixie's Land, where I was born in,
Early on one frosty mornin'.
Look away, look away, look away Dixie Land!

I wish I was in Dixie, Hooray! Hooray!
In Dixie's Land I'll take my stand,
To live and die in Dixie.
Away, away, away down south in Dixie!
Away, away, away down south in Dixie!

There's buckwheat cakes and Injun batter,
Makes you fat or a little fatter.
Look away, look away, look away, Dixie Land!

Then hoe it down and scratch your gravel,
To Dixie's Land I'm bound to travel.
Look away, look away, look away, Dixie Land!

I wish I was in Dixie, Hooray! Hooray!
In Dixie's Land I'll take my stand,
To live and die in Dixie.
Away, away, away down south in Dixie!
Away, away, away down south in Dixie!

Also known as 'I Wish I Was in Dixie', the song originated from the blackface minstrel shows of the 1850s, and Daniel Decatur Emmett, known as the founder of the first troupe of blackface minstrels, is usually credited with its composition. During the American Civil War it was adopted as the Confederates' unofficial anthem, sometimes with adapted lyrics. The Unionists produced their own version and other parodies also exist. Nowadays, the song's theme is sometimes viewed as offensive, suggesting sympathy for slavery or segregation.

THE WILD ROVER

I've been a wild rover for many long year,
I've spent all my money on wine, ale and beer,
Now to give up all roving, put my money in store,
And ne'er will I play the wild rover no more.

CHORUS:
(And it's) Nay, no never, nay, no never no more,
Will I play the wild rover, no never no more.

I went into an alehouse where I used to frequent,
And I told the landlady my money was all spent,
I called for a pint but she says to me, 'Nay
Such customer as you I can meet every day.'

CHORUS

> I put my hand in my pocket, drew handfuls of gold,
> And on the round table it glittered and rolled,
> 'Now here's my best brandies, my whiskey and all.'
> 'Begone, landlady, I'll have none at all.'

CHORUS

> Now I'll go home to my parents, tell them what I've done,
> And ask to give pardon to a prodigal son,
> And if they forgive me, which they've done times before,
> Then ne'er will I play the wild rover no more.

CHORUS

'The Wild Rover' is known as a traditional Irish song but Cecil Sharp recorded it in Norfolk, around 1900. There are earlier references dating back to the sixteenth century, and it may have been known among the crews of Atlantic fishing boats. Certainly the song spread widely to Ireland, Scotland, America and even Australia. There is some suggestion that far from celebrating a dissolute life, the song originated with the Temperance movement as a warning against the perils of alcohol.

THE WILD COLONIAL BOY

> There was a wild colonial boy,
> Jack Duggan was his name.
> He was born and raised in Ireland,
> In a place called Castlemaine.

He was his father's only son,
His mother's pride and joy,
And dearly did his parents love,
The Wild Colonial Boy.

At the early age of sixteen years,
He left his native home,
And to Australia's sunny shore,
He was inclined to roam.
He robbed the rich, he helped the poor,
He shot James MacEvoy,
A terror to Australia was,
The Wild Colonial Boy.

One morning on the prairie,
As Jack he rode along,
A-listening to the mocking bird,
A-singing a cheerful song,
Up stepped a band of troopers:
Kelly, Davis and Fitzroy,
They all set out to capture him,
The Wild Colonial Boy.

Surrender now, Jack Duggan,
For you see we're three to one.
Surrender in the Queen's high name,
You are a plundering son.
Jack drew two pistols from his belt,
He proudly waved them high.
'I'll fight, but not surrender,'
Said the Wild Colonial Boy.

He fired a shot at Kelly,
Which brought him to the ground,
And turning round to Davis,
He received a fatal wound.
A bullet pierced his proud young heart,
From the pistol of Fitzroy,
And that was how they captured him,
The Wild Colonial Boy.

There are countless versions of this Irish/Australian ballad. The original was banned for being too seditious and featured an Irish rebel called Jack Donohoe. In 1825 Donohoe was transported as a convict to Australia where he became a bushranger, robbing the wealthy around Sydney. He was finally caught in a police ambush and shot dead near Campbelltown in 1830.

❦ WALTZING MATILDA ❧

Once a jolly swagman camped by a billabong,
Under the shade of a coolibah tree,
And he sang as he watched and waited till his billy boil,
You'll come a Waltzing Matilda with me.

Waltzing Matilda, Waltzing Matilda,
You'll come a Waltzing Matilda with me,
And he sang as he watched and waited till his billy boil,
You'll come a Waltzing Matilda with me.

Down came a jumbuck to drink at that billabong,
Up jumped the swagman and grabbed him with glee,
And he sang as he shoved that jumbuck in his tucker bag,
You'll come a Waltzing Matilda with me.

Waltzing Matilda, Waltzing Matilda,
You'll come a Waltzing Matilda with me,
And he sang as he shoved that jumbuck in his tucker bag,
You'll come a Waltzing Matilda with me.

Up rode the squatter mounted on his thorough-bred,
Down came the troopers one, two, three,
Whose that jolly jumbuck you've got in your tucker bag,
You'll come a Waltzing Matilda with me.

Waltzing Matilda, Waltzing Matilda,
You'll come a Waltzing Matilda with me,
Whose that jolly jumbuck you've got in your tucker bag,
You'll come a Waltzing Matilda with me.

Up jumped the swagman and sprang into the billabong,
You'll never catch me alive said he,
And his ghost may be heard as you pass by that billabong,
You'll come a Waltzing Matilda with me.

Waltzing Matilda, Waltzing Matilda,
You'll come a Waltzing Matilda with me,
And his ghost may be heard as you pass by that billabong,
You'll come a Waltzing Matilda with me.

A 'matilda' is Australian slang for the swag bag carried by travelling labourers and the song tells the sad story of an unfortunate swagman, resting under a eucalyptus (coolibah) tree. He is caught poaching a sheep (jumbuck) to eat and drowns himself in the billabong rather than face arrest when the landowner (squatter) and police arrive.

The words were written in 1895 by the Australian bush poet A. B. Paterson, better known as Banjo, and the song itself has attracted so many stories that it has its own museum in Queensland, Australia, and there is even a Waltzing Matilda Day on 6 April to commemorate the first performance. It is also Australia's unofficial national anthem.

GOD SAVE THE QUEEN

God save our gracious Queen!
Long live our noble Queen!
God save the Queen!
Send her victorious,
Happy and glorious,
Long to reign over us,
God save the Queen.

Thy choicest gifts in store
On her be pleased to pour,
Long may she reign.
May she defend our laws,
And ever give us cause,
To sing with heart and voice,
God save the Queen.

This patriotic song, which substitutes 'King' for 'Queen' when appropriate, was first performed in London in 1745 although it may date back to the seventeenth century. It was played at the Theatre Royal, Drury Lane, when George II was King and the idea quickly caught on. It soon became the custom for the song to greet the sovereign whenever he or she arrived. It was adopted as the British National Anthem at the beginning of the nineteenth century. Surprisingly, there is no authorized version of the lyrics and there were extra verses written after these original two. They are seldom sung and more contentious in content, including lines like 'Frustrate their knavish tricks' and even 'Rebellious Scots to crush'. Around 140 composers, including Bach, Beethoven and Elgar, have used the tune in their work.

AMERICA THE BEAUTIFUL

O beautiful for spacious skies,
For amber waves of grain,
For purple mountain majesties,
Above the fruited plain!
America! America!
God shed his grace on thee,
And crown thy good, with brotherhood,
From sea to shining sea!

O beautiful for pilgrim feet,
Whose stern impassioned stress,
A thoroughfare of freedom beat,

Across the wilderness!
America! America!
God mend thine every flaw,
Confirm thy soul in self-control,
Thy liberty in law!

O beautiful for heroes proved,
In liberating strife,
Who more than self, their country loved,
And mercy more than life!
America! America!
May God thy gold refine,
Till all success be nobleness,
And every gain divine!

O beautiful for patriot dream,
That sees beyond the years,
Thine alabaster cities gleam,
Undimmed by human tears!
America! America!
God shed his grace on thee,
And crown thy good, with brotherhood,
From sea to shining sea!

Katherine Lee Bates wrote the original poem called 'Pikes Peak' in 1893 as a celebration of the Fourth of July. Church organist and choirmaster Samuel A. Ward wrote the music, and poem and tune were combined and published in 1910 as 'America the Beautiful'. It has remained a hugely popular patriotic song, in many ways rivalling 'The Star-Spangled Banner', the US national anthem. There are several slightly different versions of the lyrics.

CHAPTER 3

If You Love Me,
Dilly, Dilly:
Songs of Love & Loss

Love is perhaps the most popular theme for folk lyrics and it runs through many songs in a range of guises. The search for true love, the excitement of the chase and forsaken lovers both male and female all feature. These songs tend to be melancholy in tone often mourning love's loss for a variety of reasons from the vagaries of fate, to love triangles and faithless lovers.

❧ LAVENDER'S BLUE ❧

Lavender's blue, dilly dilly, lavender's green,
When I am king, dilly, dilly, you shall be queen.
Who told you so, dilly, dilly, who told you so?
'Twas my own heart, dilly, dilly, that told me so.
Call up your men, dilly, dilly, set them to work
Some to the plow, dilly dilly, some to the fork,
Some to the hay, dilly, dilly, some to thresh corn,
While you and I, dilly, dilly, keep ourselves warm.

Lavender's green, dilly, dilly, lavender's blue,
If you love me, dilly, dilly, I will love you.
Let the birds sing, dilly, dilly, and the lambs play;
We shall be safe, dilly, dilly, out of harm's way.
I love to dance, dilly, dilly, I love to sing;
When I am queen, dilly, dilly, you'll be my king.
Who told you so, dilly, dilly, who told you so?
I told myself, dilly, dilly, I told me so.

As with many old folk songs, there are a number of different
versions and the tune probably predates the words. Earlier
lyrics printed in a seventeenth-century English broadside
were far less innocent, telling a tale of sex and drinking. It
was the Victorians who cleaned it up to make it suitable as a
children's rhyme.

❧ MADAM, WILL YOU WALK? ❧

'I should like to buy thee a fine lace cap,
With five yards of ribbon to hang down thy back,
If thou wilt walk with me.'

'I will not accept of the fine lace cap,
With the five yards of ribbon to hang down my back,
Nor I will not walk with thee.'

'I will buy thee a fine silken gown,
With nine yards of ribbon to trail upon the ground,
If thou wilt walk with me.'

'I will not accept of the fine silken gown,
With nine yards of ribbon to trail upon the ground,
Nor I won't walk with thee.'

'I'll buy thee a fine golden chair,
To sit in the garden and to take the pleasant air,
If thou wilt walk with me.'

'I will not accept of thy fine golden chair,
To sit in the garden and to take the pleasant air,
Nor I will not walk with thee.'

'I will give thee the keys of my chest,
To take gold and silver when thou art distressed,
If thou wilt walk with me.'

'I will not accept of the keys of your chest,
To take gold and silver when I am distressed,
Nor I will not walk with thee.'

'I'll give thee the key, Oh the key of my heart,
And thy heart and my heart shall never depart,
If thou wilt walk with me.'

'I will accept of the key of your heart,
And thy heart and my heart shall never depart,
And I will walk with thee.'

A traditional male-female courtship song that was sometimes sung in two teams, 'Madam, Will You Walk?' was included in Halliwell's book of rhymes in 1849 but is almost certainly older than that. Although originally an English folk song, it was widely known throughout Great Britain and also in the Appalachian Mountain region of America where early settlers, who were mainly Scots-Irish, English and German, brought their musical traditions with them.

ALL AROUND MY HAT

CHORUS:
All around my hat, I will wear the green willow,
And all around my hat, for a twelve-month and a day.
And if anyone should ask me the reason why I'm wearing it,
It's all for my true love, who's far, far away.

My love she was fair, and my love she was handsome,
And cruel were the judges that sentenced her away.
For thieving was a thing that she never was inclined to,
They sent my love across the sea ten thousand miles
    away.

CHORUS

Seven long, long years my love and I are parted,
Seven long, long years they've sentenced her away.
Seven long years I'll love my love and never be false-
    hearted,
And never sigh or sorrow though she's far, far away.

CHORUS

Some young men are false and they're full of all
    deceiving,
Seeking for some young girl they mean to lead astray.
And when they have deceived them, so cruelly they
    leave them,
But I'll love my love forever though she's far, far away.

CHORUS

Willow represents sorrow, from weeping willow, and 'twelve-month and a day' is probably a reference to mourning and ancient betrothal vows.

The version above is the original nineteenth-century folk song about a street hawker's lament for his lost love, a cockney flower girl caught stealing and sentenced to transportation to Australia, ten thousand miles away. The lyrics were also adapted as an Irish rebel song after the Easter Rising of 1916. Steeleye Span made a different version famous with the release of his single in 1975 but the verses were largely taken from another song called *Farewell He*:

It is fare thee well, cold winter, it is fare thee well, cold
　　frost;
There is nothing I have gained, but a lover I have lost,
I will sing and I'll be merry, and I'll clap my hands with
　　glee,
And I'll rest me when I'm weary: let him go then,
　　farewell he.

It was last fall that my lover gave to me a diamond ring,
O, I know not what he thought me but a vain and foolish
　　thing,
If he prove to me unskilful, cannot win my heart from me,
I will prove a maiden wilful: let him go with – farewell he.

If he has another sweetheart and tells me so in joke,
Why I care not, be they twenty, he will never me provoke.
Well, and if he like another and together they agree,
I can also find a lover, let him go with – farewell he.

Add half a pound of reason, half an ounce of common
　　sense,
Add a sprig of thyme in season as much of sage prudence,
Prithee mix them well together, then I think you'll
　　plainly see,
He's no lad for windy weather; let him go with –
　　farewell he.

❦ YE BANKS AND BRAES ❧
O' BONNIE DOON

Ye banks and braes o' bonnie Doon,
How can ye bloom sae fresh and fair?
How can ye chant, ye little birds,
And I'm sae weary, fu' o' care!
Ye'll break my heart, ye warbling bird,
That wantons through the flow'ring thorn,
Ye mind me o' departed joys,
Departed never to return.

Oft ha'e I roved by bonnie Doon,
To see the rose and woodbine twine;
And ilka bird sang o' its luve,
And fondly sae did I o' mine.
Wi' lightsome heart I stretch'd my hand,
And pu'd a rosebud from the tree;
But my fause lover stole the rose,
And left, and left the thorn wi' me.

Robert Burns wrote the lyrics in 1791. The Doon flows from
Loch Doon to the Firth of Clyde, past Burns' hometown of
Alloway. He also mentions the river in his poem 'Tam O'
Shanter'. James Miller, a clerk at the General Register House
in Edinburgh, composed the melody as 'The Caledonian
Hunt's Delight' having been advised by his friend Stephen
Clark to 'keep to the black keys of the harpsichord and main-
tain some kind of rhythm'. It was Clark who suggested the
tune to Burns.

❦ COCKLES AND MUSSELS ❧

In Dublin's fair city,
Where the girls are so pretty,
I first set my eyes on sweet Molly Malone,
As she wheeled her wheel-barrow,
Through streets broad and narrow,
Crying, 'Cockles and mussels, alive, alive, oh!'

CHORUS:
'Alive, alive, oh,
Alive, alive, oh,'
Crying, 'Cockles and mussels, alive, alive, oh!'

She was a fishmonger,
But sure 'twas no wonder,
For so were her father and mother before,
And they wheeled their barrows,
Through the streets broad and narrow,
Crying, 'Cockles and mussels, alive, alive, oh!'

CHORUS

She died of a fever,
And no one could save her,
And that was the end of sweet Molly Malone.
But her ghost wheels her barrow,
Through streets broad and narrow,
Crying, 'Cockles and mussels, alive, alive, oh!'

CHORUS

Molly Malone is commemorated by a statue in Dublin's Grafton Street, although it has temporarily been moved to outside the tourist office in Suffolk Street. The statue, designed by Jeanne Rynhart, was unveiled in 1988 and 13 June was declared Molly Malone day. The character is fictional although a story was widely circulated that she was a real person who worked as a barrow girl by day and a prostitute at night. Molly Malone was said to have died on 13 June 1699. The song first appeared in print in 1888, in Cambridge, Massachusetts.

❧ THE MAID OF LLANWELLYN ☙

I've no sheep on the mountains,
Nor boat on the lake,
Nor coin in my coffer,
To keep me awake,
Nor corn in my garner,
Nor fruit on my tree,
Yet the maid of Llanwellyn
Smiles sweetly on me.

Soft tapping, at eve,
To her window I came,
And loud bayed the watch-dog,
Loud scolded the dame,

For shame, silly Lightfoot,
What is it to thee,
Though the maid of Llanwellyn
Smiles sweetly on me?

Rich Owen will tell you,
With eyes full of scorn,
Threadbare is my coat,
And my hosen are torn,
Scoff on, my rich Owen,
For faint is thy glee,
When the maid of Llanwellyn
Smiles sweetly on me.

The farmer rides proudly,
To market and fair,
And the clerk at the ale house,
Still claims the great chair,
But of all our proud fellows,
The proudest I'll be,
While the maid of Llanwellyn
Smiles sweetly on me.

For blithe as the urchin,
At holiday play,
And meek as the matron,
In mantle of gray,
And trim as the lady,
Of gentle degree,
Is the maid of Llanwellyn
Who smiles upon me.

The lyrics were written by Joanna Baillie and published by George Thompson of Edinburgh in the early nineteenth century. When Thompson (clearly a pedant regarding linguistics) pointed out that Wales had no lakes, Baillie adamantly refused to change the line, saying they must just 'hope that their readers would be as ignorant as she had been when she wrote it'. Thompson was the organizer and director of the first Edinburgh Music Festival and a collector of folk songs. He had previously paid both Haydn and Beethoven to write 'improved' tunes for older British songs.

OH MY DARLING, CLEMENTINE

In a cavern, in a canyon,
Excavating for a mine,
Dwelt a miner, forty-niner,
And his daughter, Clementine.

CHORUS:
Oh my darling, Oh my darling,
Oh my darling, Clementine.
You are lost and gone forever,
Dreadful sorry, Clementine.

Light she was and like a fairy,
And her shoes were number nine,
Herring boxes without topses,
Sandals were for Clementine.

CHORUS

> Drove she ducklings, to the water,
> Every morning just at nine,
> Hit her foot against a splinter,
> Fell into the foaming brine.

CHORUS

> Ruby lips above the water,
> Blowing bubbles soft and fine,
> But alas I was no swimmer,
> Neither was my Clementine.

CHORUS

> In a churchyard near the canyon,
> Where the myrtle doth entwine,
> There grow roses and the posies,
> Fertilized by Clementine.

CHORUS

> Then the miner, forty-niner,
> Soon began to peak and pine,
> Thought he oughter join his daughter,
> Now he's with his Clementine.

CHORUS

> I'm so lonely, lost without her,
> Wish I'd had a fishing line,
> Which I might have cast about her,
> Might have saved my Clementine.

CHORUS

In my dreams she still doth haunt me,
Robed in garments, soaked in brine,
Then she rises from the waters,
And I kiss my Clementine.

CHORUS

How I missed her! How I missed her!
How I missed my Clementine,
But I kissed her little sister,
And forgot my Clementine.

This folk ballad from the American West at first appears to be a sad tale. In fact it is a parody of a lover's lament after the tragi-comic death of his sweetheart, the daughter of a miner from the 1849 Californian gold rush. It is usually attributed to Percy Montrose around 1880 and it may have originated from a tune called 'Down by the River Lived a Maiden', written in 1863 by H. S. Thompson, another American songwriter.

❧ OH NO, JOHN! ☙

On yonder hill there stands a creature,
Who she is I do not know.
I'll go and court her for her beauty,
She must answer yes or no.
Oh no, John! No John! No John! No!

On her bosom are bunches of posies,
On her breast where flowers grow.

If I should chance to touch that posy,
She must answer yes or no.
Oh no, John! No John! No John! No!

Madam I am come for to court you,
If your favour I can gain.
If you will but entertain me,
Perhaps then I might come again.
Oh no, John! No John! No John! No!

My husband was a Spanish captain,
Went to sea a month ago.
The very last time we kissed and parted,
Bid me always answer no.
Oh no, John! No John! No John! No!

Madam in your face is beauty,
In your bosom flowers grow.
In your bedroom there is pleasure,
Shall I view it, yes or no?
Oh no, John! No John! No John! No!

Madam shall I tie your garter,
Tie it a little above your knee?
If my hand should slip a little farther,
Would you think it amiss of me?
Oh no, John! No John! No John! No!

My love and I went to bed together,
There we lay till cocks did crow.
Unclose your arms my dearest jewel,
Unclose your arms and let me go.
Oh no, John! No John! No John! No!

A rather more innocent version became popular after Cecil Sharp, the collector of folk music, published it in *Folk Songs from Somerset* in 1908. He thought this original was 'coarse' and revised the lines to make them suitable for schoolchildren. The song probably developed from an old English singing game.

❧ BUFFALO GALS ☙

As I was walking down the street,
Down the street, down the street,
A pretty little gal I chanced to meet,
Oh, she was fair to view.

CHORUS:
Buffalo gals won't you come out tonight,
Come out tonight, come out tonight.
Buffalo gals won't you come out tonight,
And dance by the light of the moon.

She was the prettiest gal I've seen in my life,
In my life, in my life,
And I wished to the Lord she'd be my wife,
Then we would part no more.

CHORUS

Oh, yes, dear boy, I'm coming out tonight,
Coming out tonight, coming out tonight,

Oh, yes, dear boy, I'm coming out tonight,
And we'll dance by the light of the moon.

CHORUS

I danced with that gal with a hole in her stocking,
And her heel kept a-rockin' and her toe kept a-knockin',
I danced with that gal with a hole in her stocking,
And we danced by the light of the moon.

CHORUS

Originally called 'Lubly Fan', this traditional American song was first published in 1844. It quickly became popular and various town and state names were linked to it, including Charleston, Alabama and New York, but Buffalo was the one that stuck. The blackface minstrel John Hodges, who performed as 'Cool White', is sometimes credited with the lyrics but they were most likely adapted from other material.

WHEN YOU AND I WERE YOUNG, MAGGIE

I wandered today to the hill, Maggie,
To watch the scene below,
The creek and the creaking old mill, Maggie,
As we used to, long ago.
The green grove is gone for the hill, Maggie,
Where first the daisies sprung;

The creaking old mill is still, Maggie,
Since you and I were young.

CHORUS:
And now we are aged and grey, Maggie,
And the trials of life nearly done,
Let us sing of the days that are gone, Maggie,
When you and I were young.

A city so silent and lone, Maggie,
Where the young, and the gay, and the best,
In polished white mansions of stone, Maggie,
Have each found a place of rest,
Is built where the birds used to play, Maggie,
And join in the songs that we sung;
For we sang as lovely as they, Maggie,
When you and I were young.

CHORUS

They say that I'm feeble with age, Maggie,
My steps are less sprightly than then,
My face is a well-written page, Maggie,
And time alone was the pen,
They say we are aged and grey, Maggie,
As sprays by the white breakers flung;
But to me you're as fair as you were, Maggie,
When you and I were young.

CHORUS

George Johnson, a Canadian schoolteacher from Toronto, wrote the lyrics in 1864, standing on a hill above Niagara, overlooking the town of Hamilton. Maggie was his fiancée, Margaret Clark, a former pupil, and she was seriously ill with tuberculosis. They were married later that year, but sadly she died in May 1865. The poem was published in Johnson's book *Maple Leaves*, and his friend J. C. Butterfield set it to music. The song became so popular that a plaque commemorating the pair stands in front of the schoolhouse where they met.

SHE'S LIKE THE SWALLOW

She's like the swallow that flies so high,
She's like the river that never runs dry.
She's like the sunshine on the lee shore,
She loves her love but she'll love no more.

'Twas down in the meadow this fair maid bent,
A-picking the primrose just as she went.
The more she picked and the more she pulled,
Until she gathered her apron full.

She climbed on yonder hill above,
To give a rose unto her love.
She gave him one, she gave him three,
She gave her heart for company.

And as they sat on yonder hill,
His heart grew hard, so harder still.

He has two hearts instead of one,
She says, 'Young man, what have you done?'

'How foolish, foolish you must be,
To think I love no one but thee.
The world's not made for one alone,
I take delight in everyone.'

She took her roses and made a bed,
A stony pillow for her head.
She lay her down, no more did say,
But let her roses fade away.

She's like the swallow that flies so high,
She's like the river that never runs dry.
She's like the sunshine on the lee shore,
She loves her love but she'll love no more.

This old Canadian folk song was first written down by Maud Karpeles in 1930 and arranged for piano and singer by Vaughan Williams in 1934. This particular version of the lyrics was collected by Kenneth Peacock in 1959. It tells the sad tale of a young girl who falls in love but is abandoned by her lover when she becomes pregnant and ends with her taking her own life. The ballad's origins may lie in England but the words are from Newfoundland, which in the 1930s was still a self-governing collection of small fishing communities.

❦ DRINK TO ME ONLY ❧
WITH THINE EYES

Drink to me only with thine eyes,
And I will pledge with mine;
Or leave a kiss but in the cup,
And I'll not look for wine.
The thirst that from the soul doth rise
Doth ask a drink divine;
But might I of Jove's nectar sup,
I would not change for thine.

I sent thee late a rosy wreath,
Not so much honouring thee
As giving it a hope, that there
It could not withered be.
But though thereon didst only breathe,
And sent'st it back to me;
Since when it grows, and smells, I swear,
Not of itself, but thee.

The words for this popular English song are taken from Ben
Jonson's poem, 'Song: To Celia', which he wrote in 1616. The
poem has many parallels with classical literature including
Catullus and the Epistles of Philostratus, and this is the best
known of Jonson's work. The melody was probably composed
later in the eighteenth century.

❧ BLACK IS THE COLOUR ❧
OF MY TRUE LOVE'S HAIR

But black is the colour of my true love's hair,
His face is like some rosy fair,
The prettiest face and the neatest hands,
I love the ground whereon he stands.

I love my love and well he knows,
I love the ground whereon he goes,
If you no more on earth I see,
I can't serve you as you have me.

The winter's passed and the leaves are green,
The time is passed that we have seen,
But still I hope the time will come,
When you and I shall be as one.

I go to the Clyde for to mourn and weep,
But satisfied I never could sleep.
I'll write to you a few short lines,
I'll suffer death ten thousand times.

So fare you well, my own true love,
The time has passed, but I wish you well.
But still I hope the time will come,
When you and I will be as one.

I love my love and well he knows,
I love the ground whereon he goes.

The prettiest face, the neatest hands,
I love the ground whereon he stands.

The reference to the Clyde suggests this folk song is Scottish, but it was first recorded in the Appalachian Mountain region of the USA in 1915. There are many versions, some sung from a female viewpoint and some from a male. There are also two different tunes: one traditional melody and the second written by the Kentucky composer and singer John Jacob Niles in 1941.

CHAPTER 4

Dirty No-Good Robbing Maggie May: A Fool for Love

Lust, marital infidelity and trickery often result in lively, comedic songs. Bad behaviour also earns its just reward with the sinner duly punished or sent away, driving home the message that immorality carries consequences. The Victorian and Edwardian vogue for virtue, or at least the appearance of it, meant that many songs' originally bawdy lyrics were somewhat sanitized when written down by song collectors.

❧ SOLDIER, SOLDIER, ⅋ WON'T YOU MARRY ME?

Oh soldier, soldier, won't you marry me
With your musket, fife and drum?
Oh no sweet maid, I cannot marry you
For I have no coat to put on.
So up she went to her grandfather's chest
And she brought him a coat of the very, very best.
And the soldier put it on.

Oh soldier, soldier, won't you marry me
With your musket, fife and drum?
Oh no sweet maid, I cannot marry you
For I have no hat to put on.
So up she went to her grandfather's chest
And she brought him a hat of the very, very best.
And the soldier put it on.

Oh soldier, soldier, won't you marry me
With your musket, fife and drum?
Oh no sweet maid, I cannot marry you
For I have no gloves to put on.
So up she went to her grandfather's chest
And she brought him a pair of the very, very best.
And the soldier put them on.

Oh soldier, soldier, won't you marry me
With your musket, fife and drum?
Oh no sweet maid, I cannot marry you

For I have no boots to put on.
So up she went to her grandfather's chest
And she brought him a pair of the very, very best.
And the soldier put them on.

Oh soldier, soldier, won't you marry me
With your musket, fife and drum?
Oh no sweet maid, I cannot marry you
For I have a wife of my own.

This is the sad tale of an innocent duped by a cad, in this case a soldier, out for what he can get. Some versions include extra verses for trousers and shirt, though none offer an epilogue telling what the sweet maid does next. It is probably not very old and first appeared in a collection of traditional songs at the beginning of the twentieth century.

❧ EARLY ONE MORNING ❧

Early one morning, just as the sun was rising,
I heard a young maid sing in the valley below.
'Oh don't deceive me, oh never leave me,
How could you use a poor maiden so?

Remember the vows that you made to me truly,
Remember how tenderly you nestled close to me.
Gay is the garland, fresh are the roses
I've culled from the garden to bind over thee.

Here I now wander alone as I wonder,
Why did you leave me to sigh and complain?
I ask of the roses, why should I be forsaken,
Why must I here in sorrow remain?

Through yonder grove, by the spring that is running,
There you and I have so merrily played.
Kissing and courting and gently sporting,
Oh, my innocent heart you've betrayed.

How could you slight so a pretty girl who loves you,
A pretty girl who loves you so dearly and warm?
Though love's folly is surely but a fancy,
Still it should prove to me sweeter than your scorn.

Soon you will meet with another pretty maiden,
Some pretty maiden, you'll court her for a while.
Thus ever ranging, turning and changing,
Always seeking for a girl that is new.'

Thus sang the maiden, her sorrows bewailing,
Thus sang the maiden in the valley below.
'Oh don't deceive me, oh never leave me,
How could you use a poor maiden so?'

Another sad song lamenting the loss of a deceiving lover. The words were well known by the end of the eighteenth century, with early versions called 'The Lamenting Maid' or 'The Lovesick Maid', although the wording varies after the opening lines. They were printed with the melody in London music publisher William Chappell's collection of *National English Airs* in the mid-nineteenth century.

❧ GREENSLEEVES ❧

Alas, my love, you do me wrong
To cast me off discourteously;
And I have loved you so long,
Delighting in your company.

CHORUS:

> *Greensleeves was all my joy,*
> *Greensleeves was my delight;*
> *Greensleeves was my heart of gold,*
> *And who but my Lady Greensleeves?*

I have been ready at your hand,
To grant whatever you would crave;
I have both waged life and land,
Your love and goodwill for to have.

CHORUS

I bought thee kerchers to thy head,
That were wrought fine and gallantly;
I kept thee both at board and bed,
Which cost my purse well favouredly.

CHORUS

I bought thee petticoats of the best,
The cloth so fine as fine might be;
I gave thee jewels for thy chest,
And all this cost I spent on thee.

CHORUS

> Thy purse and eke thy gay gilt knives,
> Thy pincase gallant to the eye;
> No better wore the burgess wives,
> And yet thou wouldst not love me.

CHORUS

> Thy gown was of the grassy green,
> Thy sleeves of satin hanging by,
> Which made thee be our harvest queen,
> And yet thou wouldst not love me.

CHORUS

> My gayest gelding I thee gave,
> To ride wherever liked thee;
> No lady ever was so brave,
> And yet thou wouldst not love me.

CHORUS

> For every morning when thou rose,
> I sent thee dainties orderly,
> To cheer thy stomach from all woes,
> And yet though wouldst not love me.

CHORUS

> Well, I will pray to God on high,
> That though my constancy mayst see,
> And that yet once before I die,
> Thou wilt vouchsafe to love me.

CHORUS

Greensleeves, now farewell, adieu!
God I pray to prosper thee;
For I am still thy lover true,
Come once again and love me.

CHORUS

On this occasion the spurned lover is a man, declaring his enduring love for a cold mistress upon whom he lavished gifts and attention. It is a popular belief that 'Greensleeves' was composed by Henry VIII for Anne Boleyn, although the style makes it more likely to be Elizabethan and the first written reference dates from 1580. The song is mentioned by Shakespeare, suggesting it was a common favourite by the turn of the seventeenth century. The colour green could be seen as an allusion to promiscuity, indicating grass stains on a woman's dress; however, it was also a fashionable colour for ladies of the court and in France symbolized true love.

LOVELY JOAN

A fine young man it was indeed,
He was mounted on his milk-white steed.
He rode, he rode, himself all alone
Until he came to lovely Joan.

'Good morning to you, pretty maid.'
And 'Twice good morning, sir,' she said.

He gave her a wink, and she rolled her eye.
Says he to himself, 'I'll be there by and by.'

'Oh, don't you think these pooks of hay
A pretty place for us to play?
So come with me like a sweet young thing,
And I'll give you my golden ring.'

Then he pulled off his ring of gold,
'My pretty little miss, do this behold,
I'd freely give it for your maidenhead.'
And her cheeks they blushed like the roses red.

'Give me that ring into my hand
And I would neither stay nor stand.
For this would do more good to me
Than twenty maidenheads,' said she.

And as he made for the pooks of hay,
She leapt on his horse and tore away.
He called, he called, but it was all in vain,
Young Joan she never looked back again.

She didn't think herself quite safe
Not till she came to her true love's gate.
She'd robbed him of his horse and ring
And left him to rage in the meadows green.

This traditional English song was sung to Ralph Vaughan Williams in a Norfolk pub in 1908 by a farm labourer called Christopher Jay. Vaughan Williams later published the song in *The Penguin Book of English Folk Songs*, which he compiled with A. L. Lloyd, and used the tune in his Fantasia on 'Greensleeves'. Unlike many of its contemporaries, this song has an innocent who is rather more cunning and makes a fool of her would-be seducer.

❧ MYFANWY ☙

Why is it anger, O Myfanwy,
That fills your eyes so dark and clear?
Your gentle cheeks, O sweet Myfanwy,
Why blush they not when I draw near?
Where is the smile that once most tender
Kindled my love so fond, so true?
Where is the sound of your sweet words,
That drew my heart to follow you?

What have I done, O my Myfanwy,
To earn your frown? What is my blame?
Was it just play, my sweet Myfanwy,
To set your poet's love aflame?
You truly once to me were promised,
Is it too much to keep your part?
I wish no more your hand, Myfanwy,
If I no longer have your heart.

Myfanwy, may you spend your lifetime
Beneath the midday sunshine's glow,
And on your cheeks O may the roses
Dance for a hundred years or so.
Forget now all the words of promise
You made to one who loved you well,
Give me your hand, my sweet Myfanwy,
But one last time, to say 'farewell'.

IN THE ORIGINAL WELSH

Paham mae dicter, O Myfanwy,
Yn llenwi'th lygaid duon di?
A'th ruddiau tirion, O Myfanwy,
Heb wrido wrth fy ngweled i?
Pa le mae'r wen oedd ar dy wefus
Fu'n cynnau 'nghariad ffyddion ffol?
Pa le mae sain dy eiriau melys,
Fu'n denu'n nghalon ar dy ol?

Pa beth a wneuthum, O Myfanwy
I haeddu gwg dy ddwyrudd hardd?
Ai chwarae oeddit, O Myfanwy
A thanau euraidd serch dy fardd?
Wyt eiddo im drwy gywir amod
Ai gormod cadw'th air i mi?
Ni cheisiaf fyth mo'th law, Myfanwy,
Heb gael dy gallon gyda hi.

Myfanwy boed yr holl o'th fywyd
Dan heulwen ddisglair canol dydd.
A boed i rosyn gwridog iechyd
I ddawnsio ganmlwydd ar dy rudd.

Anghofia'r oll o'th addewidion
A wneist I rywun, 'ngeneth ddel,
A dyro'th law, Myfanwy dirion
I ddim ond dweud y gair 'Ffarwel'.

Joseph Parry wrote the music and Richard Davies the lyrics. It is sometimes said to be about Parry's childhood sweetheart Myfanwy Llewellyn but was more likely inspired by Hywel ap Einion's poem to his lost love Myfanwy Ferch Tudor Trefor, written around 1350. She was the daughter of the Earl of Arundel and said to have been the most beautiful woman in Powys. This popular song was first published in 1875.

THE FOGGY DEW

When I was a bachelor, I lived all alone,
And worked at the weaver's trade,
And the only, only thing that I did that was wrong,
Was to woo a fair young maid.
I wooed her in the summertime,
And part of the winter, too,
And all night long I held her in my arms
Just to keep her from the foggy, foggy dew.

One night she came to my bedside,
When I was fast asleep,
She threw her arms around my neck,
And bitterly did weep.

She wept, she cried, she damn near died,
Poor me what could I do?
So all night long I held her in my arms
Just to keep her from the foggy, foggy dew.

Again, I am a bachelor and I live with my son,
We work at the weaver's trade.
And every time I look into his eyes,
He reminds me of that fair young maid.
He reminds me of the summertime,
And part of the winter, too,
And of the many, many times I held her in my arms
Just to keep her from the foggy dew.

Originally an English song, 'The Foggy Dew' was first published in a broadside around 1815. When he was collecting folk songs in the early twentieth century, Cecil Sharp found at least eight different versions. It was also popular in the US and Burl Ives who recorded it in the 1940s claimed that there was a colonial American version. There is also a completely different Irish rebel song of the same name.

MAGGIE MAY

Now gather round you sailor boys and listen to my plea
And when you've heard my tale you'll pity me:
For I was a real damned fool in the port of Liverpool
The first time that I came home from the sea.

I was paid off at the Home, from a voyage to Sierra Leone:
Two pounds ten and sixpence was my pay.
When I drew the tin I grinned, but I very soon got skinned
By a girl by the name of Maggie May.

CHORUS:

Oh, dirty Maggie May, they've taken her away;
And she'll never walk down Lime Street any more.
For she robbed so many a sailor, and skinned so many a
*   whaler –*
That dirty, no-good, robbing Maggie May.

I shan't forget the day when I first met Maggie May,
She was cruising up and down on Canning Place,
With a figure so divine, like a frigate of the line,
So, being a sailor, I gave chase.

CHORUS

Next day I woke in bed, with a sore and aching head,
No shoes, or shirt, or trousers could I find.
I asked here where they were, and she answered, 'My
          dear sir,
They're down in Kelly's knock-shop, number nine.'

CHORUS

Oh, you thieving Maggie May, you robbed me of my pay
When I slept with you last night ashore;
And the judge he guilty found her, of robbing a
          homeward-bounder,
And she'll never roam down Lime Street any more.

CHORUS

This traditional song from Liverpool dates from the early nineteenth century and tells the story of a prostitute called Maggie May, or Mae, who plies her trade and robs her gullible clients before being caught and transported to Australia as punishment. The lyrics have been adapted over the years – there's even an Australian version – and other streets from the port's red-light district sometimes feature, including 'You'll never shine in Paradise Street no more.'

ALLY CROAKER

There lived a man in Ballinacasey
Who wanted a wife to make him uneasy.
Long had he sigh'd for dear Ally Croaker,
And thus the gentle youth bespoke her,
'Will you marry me, dear Ally Croaker,
Will you marry me, dear Ally, Ally Croaker?'

This artless young man just come from the schoolary,
A novice in love, and all its foolery,
Too dull for a wit, too grave for joker,
And thus the gentle youth bespoke her,
'Will you marry me, dear Ally Croaker,
 Will you marry me, dear Ally, Ally Croaker?'

He drank with the father, he talk'd with the mother,
He romp'd with the sister, he gam'd with the brother,
He gam'd, 'til he pawned his coat to the broker,
Which cost him the heart of his dear Ally Croaker,
Oh! the fickle, fickle Ally Croaker,
Oh! the fickle, fickle Ally, Ally Croaker.

To all ye young men who are fond of gaming,
Who are spending your money, whilst others are saving,
Fortune's a jilt, the devil may choke her,
A jilt more inconstant than dear Ally Croaker,
Oh! the inconstant Ally Croaker,
Oh! the inconstant Ally, Ally Croaker.

The song dates to around 1725 and was written by Lawrence Grogan of County Wexford, who was a popular 'gentleman piper' and composer of Irish airs. The lyrics tell the story of the rejected suitor of Alicia Croaker, sister of the High Sheriff of County Limerick, Edward Croker. The song quickly gained popularity in Ireland and appeared in the plays *Love in a Riddle* in 1729 and *The Englishman in Paris*, Samuel Foote's play of 1753, in which the lyrics were slightly altered.

❧ OLD SMOKEY ☙

On top of old Smokey,
All covered in snow,
I lost my true lover
From courtin' too slow.

For meetin' is pleasure,
And partin' is grief,
And a false-hearted true love
Is worse than a thief.

A thief he'll but rob you,
And take what you have,
But a false-hearted true love
Will send you to your grave.

Your grave will decay you,
And turn you to dust,
Not one boy in fifty
That a poor girl can trust.

They'll hug you and kiss you,
They'll tell you more lies,
Than crossties on a railroad
Or stars in the skies.

Just as sure as the dew falls,
All on the green corn,
Last night he was with me,
This mornin' he's gone.

This lament of a backwoods girl for her travelling wagoner sweetheart is a well-known American folk song. Old Smokey may be a mountain in the Appalachians or Ozarks where many of the settlers were of Scots-Irish descent. Pete Seeger, who recorded his own version in the 1960s, thought the song had travelled across the Atlantic and had its roots in Elizabethan ballads.

❧ THE HOUSE ❧
OF THE RISING SUN

There is a house in New Orleans,
They call the Rising Sun,
It's been the ruin of many a poor girl,
And me, O God, for one.

Go tell my baby sister,
Never do like I have done,
Tell her to shun that house in New Orleans,
They call the Rising Sun.

If I'd a listened what my mama said,
I'd-a been at home today,
Being so young and foolish, poor boy,
Let a rambler lead me astray.

My mother, she's a tailor,
She made those new blue jeans,
My sweetheart he's a drunkard, Lord, Lord,
Drinks down in New Orleans.

The only thing a drunkard needs
Is a suitcase and a trunk,
The only time he's satisfied
Is when he's on a drunk.

Fills his glasses to the brim
And passes them around,

The only pleasure he gets outa life,
Is ramblin' from town to town.

One foot is on the platform,
The other one on the train,
I'm goin' back to New Orleans,
To wear that ball and chain.

Goin' back to New Orleans,
My race is almost run,
Goin' to spend the rest of my life,
Beneath the Rising Sun.

This is the song as recorded by American folklorist Alan Lomax in Middlesboro, Kentucky, in 1937. He described Georgia Turner, the sixteen-year-old singer, as 'a ragged Kentucky Mountain girl'. Many popular recordings have followed, often sung from a male point of view. It is likely that the song originated from an older English broadside ballad, taken to America by settlers.

CHAPTER 5

Bravest Men Must Fight: Men at Arms

Armies traditionally relied on patriotism, camaraderie and a positive image to encourage recruitment. As a result these songs tend to be up-beat in tone, rousing national fervour and patriotism.

Bravery always inspired admiration and many songs remember gallant leaders, who, though defeated, continued to cut dashing figures in the public's imagination and command respect. Highwaymen, those men of arms on the wrong side of the law, also maintained a swashbuckling glamour, especially those betrayed by fickle friends or lovers.

THE STAR-SPANGLED BANNER

O! say can you see by the dawn's early light
What so proudly we hailed at the twilight's last gleaming?
Whose broad stripes and bright stars through the
    perilous fight,
O'er the ramparts we watched were so gallantly streaming?
And the rockets' red glare, the bombs bursting in air,
Gave proof through the night that our flag was still there.
O! say does that star-spangled banner yet wave
O'er the land of the free and the home of the brave?

On the shore, dimly seen through the mists of the deep,
Where the foe's haughty host in dread silence reposes,
What is that which the breeze, o'er the towering steep,
As it fitfully blows, half conceals, half discloses?
Now it catches the gleam of the morning's first beam,
In full glory reflected now shines in the stream:
'Tis the star-spangled banner! Oh long may it wave
O'er the land of the free and the home of the brave.

And where is that band who so vauntingly swore
That the havoc of war and the battle's confusion,
A home and a country should leave us no more!
Their blood has washed out their foul footsteps'
    pollution.
No refuge could save the hireling and slave
From the terror of flight, or the gloom of the grave:
And the star-spangled banner in triumph doth wave
O'er the land of the free and the home of the brave.

O! thus be it ever, when freemen shall stand
Between their loved home and war's desolation!
Blest with victory and peace, may the heav'n rescued
    land
Praise the Power that hath made and preserved us a
    nation.
Then conquer we must, when our cause it is just,
And this be our motto: 'In God is our trust.'
And the star-spangled banner in triumph shall wave
O'er the land of the free and the home of the brave!

'The Star Spangled Banner' was adopted as the American national anthem in 1931 in a congressional resolution signed by President Hoover. It was originally called 'Defence of Fort McHenry', written by Francis Scott Key after witnessing the British bombardment of Baltimore during the War of 1812. The tune by John Stafford Smith had been the official song of the Anacreontic Society, an eighteenth-century gentleman's club in London.

❧ JOHN BROWN'S BODY ❧

John Brown's body lies a-mouldering in the grave;
John Brown's body lies a-mouldering in the grave;
John Brown's body lies a-mouldering in the grave;
His soul is marching on!

CHORUS:

Glory, glory, hallelujah! Glory, glory, hallelujah!
Glory, glory, hallelujah! His soul is marching on!

He's gone to be a soldier in the army of the Lord! *(×3)*
His soul is marching on!

CHORUS

John Brown's knapsack is strapped upon his back! *(×3)*
His soul is marching on!

CHORUS

His pet lambs will meet him on the way; *(×3)*
They go marching on!

CHORUS

They will hang Jeff Davis to a sour apple tree; *(×3)*
As they march along!

CHORUS

Now, three rousing cheers for the Union; *(×3)*
As we are marching on!

Originally an American religious camp meeting song from the 1850s with the opening line, 'Say Brothers will you meet us on Canaan's happy shore', the song was adopted by the army for its good marching tempo. After the execution of the abolitionist and anti-slavery activist John Brown, in 1859, his name was included in the lyrics. The revised song spread throughout the Union Army, particularly after the outbreak of the American Civil War in 1861. There was also a rival Confederate version in which John Brown's body hung from a tree. The music was used by Julia Ward Howe as the setting for her 'Battle Hymn of the Republic' written in November 1861.

THE BATTLE HYMN OF THE REPUBLIC

Mine eyes have seen the glory of the coming of the
  Lord,
He is trampling out the vintage where the grapes of
  wrath are stored,
He hath loosed his fateful lightning of His terrible swift
  sword,
His truth is marching on.

CHORUS:
Glory! Glory! Hallelujah! Glory! Glory! Hallelujah!
Glory! Glory! Hallelujah! His truth is marching on!

I have seen Him in the watch fires of a hundred circling
camps,
They have builded Him an altar in the evening dews and
damps,
I can read His righteous sentence in the dim and daring
lamps,
His day is marching on.

CHORUS

I have read a fiery Gospel writ in burnished rows of
steel,
'As ye deal with My contemners so with you My grace
shall deal,'
Let the Hero born of woman crush the serpent with His
heel,
Since God is marching on.

CHORUS

He has sounded forth the trumpet that shall never call
retreat,
He is sitting out the hearts of men before His judgment
seat,
Oh, be swift my soul to answer Him, be jubilant, my feet,
Our God is marching on.

CHORUS

The Reverend James Freeman Clark was an American theologian and author, active in the anti-slavery movement. He challenged his fellow abolitionist Julia Ward Howe to write more powerful lyrics for the song 'John Brown's Body'. Her poem 'The Battle Hymn of the Republic' was first published in *The Atlantic Monthly* of 1862 and appeared with the original marching song in Father Kemp's *Old Folk Concert Tunes* in 1874.

❧ WHEN JOHNNY ❧ COMES MARCHING HOME

When Johnny comes marching home again,
Hurrah! Hurrah!
We'll give him a hearty welcome then,
Hurrah! Hurrah!
The men will cheer and the boys will shout,
The ladies they will all turn out,
And we'll all feel gay,
When Johnny comes marching home.

The old church bell will peal with joy,
Hurrah! Hurrah!
The village lads and lassies say,
With roses they strew the way,
And we'll all feel gay,
When Johnny comes marching home.

Get ready for the Jubilee,
Hurrah! Hurrah!
We'll give the hero three times three,
Hurrah! Hurrah!
The laurel wreath is ready now,
To place upon his loyal brow,

And we'll all feel gay,
When Johnny comes marching home.

Let love and friendship on that day,
Hurrah! Hurrah!
Their choicest pleasures then display,
Hurrah! Hurrah!
And let each one perform some part,
To fill with joy the warrior's heart,
And we'll all feel gay,
When Johnny comes marching home.

The song was written during the American Civil War by the Irish-American bandleader Patrick Gilmore. He is said to have written it for his sister Annie who was waiting for her fiancé, Union Light Artillery Captain John O'Rourke, to return from the fighting. The lyrics were published under the pseudonym Louis Lambert in 1863. Several variations of the words exist and the song has featured in a number of soundtracks for films as diverse as *Gone with the Wind, Dr Strangelove, Die Hard with a Vengeance, Monty Python and the Holy Grail* and *Antz*.

YANKEE DOODLE

Yankee Doodle came to town,
Riding on a pony;
He stuck a feather in his cap
And called it macaroni.

CHORUS:

> *Yankee Doodle keep it up,*
> *Yankee Doodle dandy;*
> *Mind the music and the step,*
> *And with the girls be handy.*

Father and I went down to camp,
Along with Cap'n Gooding,
And there we saw the men and boys
As thick as hasty pudding.

CHORUS

And there we saw a thousand men
As rich as Squire David,
And what they wasted every day,
I wish it could be saved.

CHORUS

The lasses they eat it every day,
Would keep a house a-winter,
They have so much, that I'll be bound,
They eat it when they've mind ter.

CHORUS

And there I see a swamping gun,
Large as a log of maple,
Upon a deuced little cart,
A load for father's cattle.

CHORUS

And every time they shoot it off,
It takes a horn of powder,

And makes a noise like father's gun,
Only a nation louder.

CHORUS

I went as nigh to one myself,
As 'Siah's underpinning,
And father went as nigh again,
I thought the deuce was in him.

CHORUS

Cousin Simon grew so bold,
I thought he would have cocked it,
It scared me so I shrinked it off,
And hung by father's pocket.

CHORUS

And Cap'n Davis had a gun,
He kind of clapt his hand on't,
And stuck a crooked stabbing iron
Upon the little end on't.

CHORUS

And there I see a pumpkin shell,
As big as mother's basin,
And every time they touched it off,
They scampered like the nation.

CHORUS

I see a little barrel, too,
The heads were made of leather,
They knocked on it with little clubs,
And called the folks together.

CHORUS

And there was Cap'n Washington,
And gentle folks about him,
They say he's grown so 'tarnal proud,
He will not ride without 'em.

CHORUS

He got him on his meeting clothes,
Upon a slapping stallion,
He sat the world along in rows,
In hundreds and in millions.

CHORUS

The flaming ribbons in his hat,
They looked so tearing fine, ah,
I wanted dreadfully to get
To give to my Jemima.

CHORUS

I see another snarl of men,
A-digging graves they told me,
So 'tarnal long, so 'tarnal deep,
They 'tended they should hold me.

CHORUS

It scared me so, I hooked it off,
Nor stopped, as I remember,
Nor turned about till I got home,
Locked up in mother's chamber.

CHORUS

At the beginning of the American War of Independence 'Yankee Doodle' was sung by British troops to mock the American army's dishevelled appearance. A 'macaroni' was an eighteenth-century term for a young dandy who had taken the Grand Tour and wore very elaborate wigs and dressed in the European style. The inference being that the best unsophisticated Americans could manage was a feather.

After the defeat of British troops at Bunker Hill in 1775 and the Battles of Lexington and Concord, American soldiers adopted the song, adapting the words to make it their own, and this is the version we now know. They sang it to celebrate their victories, turning it against the British, who liked it a lot less once it was used to taunt them. It has remained popular in the US and is Connecticut's state song.

The tune may have been taken from a Scottish air or written as a melody without words; there's also some suggestion that 'doodle' was a way of singing. The nursery rhyme 'Lucy Locket' is sung to the same tune.

BONEY'S LAMENTATION

> Attend, you sons of high renown,
> To these few lines which I pen down:
> I was born to wear a stately crown,
> And to rule a wealthy nation.
> I am the man that beat Beaulieu,
> And Wurmser's will did then subdue;
> That great Archduke I overthrew;

On every plain my men were slain.
Grand treasures, too, I did obtain,
And got capitulation.

I did pursue the Egyptians sore,
Till Turks and Arabs lay in gore;
The rights of France I did restore
So long in confiscation.
I chased my foes through mud and mire
Till in despair my men did tire.
Then Moscow town was set on fire,
My men were lost through winter frost;
I ne'er before received such blast
Since the hour of my creation.

To Leipzig town my soldiers fled,
Montmartre was strewn with Prussian dead,
We marched them forth, inveterate,
To stop a bold invasion.
Farewell, my royal spouse, once more,
And offspring great, whom I adore!
And may you that great throne restore,
That is away, without delay!
Those kings of me have made a prey,
And caused my lamentation.

The ballad is also known as 'Boney's Abdication' with the word 'abdication' taking the place of 'lamentation' in the final line. The narrative follows Napoleon Bonaparte's career, although names and places are slightly altered, and events are not altogether in the correct order. As the song ends with Napoleon's abdication in April 1814 it was most likely written that year, before his escape from Elba in February the following year and his final defeat at the battle of Waterloo in June 1815.

❧ BONEY WAS A WARRIOR ❧

Boney was a warrior,
Way, aye, yah!
A warrior, a terrier,
Jean Francois!

Boney went to school in France,
Way, aye, yah!
He learnt to make the people dance,
Jean Francois!

Boney fought the Prussians,
Boney fought the Russians.

He beat the Prussians squarely.
He beat the British – nearly

Boney went to Elba,
Boney he came back again.

Boney went to Moscow,
Lost his army in the snow

Moscow was a-blazin',
And Boney was a-ragin'.

We beat him at Trafalgar Bay,
Blew his topmast away.

'Twas on the plains of Waterloo,
The Iron Duke he put him through.

Boney went a –cruisin',
Aboard the Billy Ruffian.

Boney went to St Helena,
An' he never came back again.

Boney broke his heart and died
On Corsica he wished he'd stayed

Boney was a general,
A rorty, snorty general.

Boney was a warrior,
Way, aye, yah!
A warrior, a terrier,
Jean Francois!

There's nothing like a victory to inspire a rousing shanty and *Boney Was a Warrior* also follows Napoleon's rise and fall, probably composed shortly after his exile and death on St Helena in 1821. A self-made man from humble origins, Napoleon was respected, even by those who had fought against him, and he became something of a folk hero, particularly in the USA and Ireland. Some versions anglicize Jean Francois to John Franswor.

MEN OF HARLECH
(*RHYFELGYRCH GWŶR HARLECH*)

Men of Harlech, march to glory,
Victory is hov'ring o'er ye,
Bright-eyed freedom stands before ye,
Hear ye not her call?
At your sloth she seems to wonder;
Rend the sluggish bonds asunder,
Let the war-cry's deaf'ning thunder
Every foe appall.
Echoes loudly waking,
Hill and valley shaking;
'Till the sound spreads wide around,
The Saxon's courage breaking;
Your foes on every side assailing,
Forward press with heart unfailing,
'Till invaders learn with quailing,
Cambria ne'er can yield!

Thou, who noble Cambria wrongest,
Know that freedom's cause is strongest,
Freedom's courage lasts the longest,
Ending but with death!
Freedom countless hosts can scatter,
Freedom stoutest mail can shatter,

Freedom thickest walls can batter,
Fate is in her breath.
See, they now are flying!
Dead are heap'd with dying!
Over might hath triumph'd right,
Our land to foes denying;
Upon their soil we never sought them,
Love of conquest hither brought them,
But this lesson we have taught them,
'Cambria ne'er can yield!'

WELSH VERSION

Wele goelcerth wen yn fflamio,
A thafodau tân yn bloeddio
Ar i'r dewrion ddod i daro,
Unwaith eto'n un:
Gan fanllefau tywysogion,
Llais gelynion, trwst arfogion,
A charlamiad y marchogion,
Craig ar graig a gryn.
Arfon byth ni orfydd,
Cenir yn dragywydd:
Cymru fydd fel Cymru fu,
Yn glodfawr ym mysg gwledydd.
Yng ngwyn oleuni'r goelcerth acw,
Tros wefusau Cymro'n marw,
Annibyniaeth sydd yn galw,
Am ei dewraf ddyn.

Ni chaiff gelyn ladd ac ymlid
Harlech! Harlech! cwyd i'w herlid
Y mae Rhoddwr mawr ein Rhyddid

Yn rhoi nerth i ni.
Wele Gymru a'i byddinoedd
Yn ymdywallt o'r mynyddoedd!
Rhuthrant fel rhaeadrau dyfroedd,
Llamant fel y lli!
Llwyddiant i'n marchogion
Rwystro gledd yr estron!
Gwybod yn ei galon gaiff,
Fel bratha cleddyf Brython;
Y cledd yn erbyn cledd a chwery,
Dur yn erbyn dur a dery,
Wele faner Gwalia'i fyny,
Rhyddid aiff â hi!

This is an early Welsh folk air and military march, said to commemorate the siege of Harlech Castle from 1461 to 1468, the longest in British history. Under the command of Dafydd ap Ieuan, the castle held out against the Yorkist king Edward IV and became a refuge for English Lancastrians. 'I held a tower in France till all the old women in Wales heard of it and now all the old women in France shall hear how I defend this castle,' Dafydd is reputed to have said.

The song has featured in many films, most famously *Zulu* in 1964, although the words were changed for the film, and it is popular with Welsh football fans as well as schools and colleges worldwide. There are a surprising number of different versions. The English lyrics printed here are by John Oxenford and were published in 1873. The Welsh lyrics are by the Welsh poet and folk-song collector John Ceiriog Hughes, published in 1890.

◆ OWAIN GLYNDŴR'S WAR SONG ◆

Saw ye the blazing star?
The Heavens look down on Freedom's war,
And light her torch on high:
Bright on the dragon crest
It tells that glory's wing shall rest,
When warriors meet to die!
Let earth's pale tyrants read despair
And vengeance in its flame,
Hail ye, my Bards! the omen fair
Of conquest and of fame,
And swell the rushing mountain air
With songs to Glyndŵr's name!

At the dead hour of night,
Marked ye how each majestic height
Burn'd in its awful beams?
Red shone th'eternal snows,
And all the land, as bright it rose,
Was full of glorious dreams.
Oh! Eagles of the battles, rise!
The hope of Gwynedd wakes:
It is your banner in the skies,
Thro' each dark cloud that breaks,
And mantles with triumphal dyes
Your thousand hills and lakes!

A sound is on the breeze,
A murmur, as of swelling seas!

The Saxon's on his way!
Lo! Spear, and shield, and lance,
From Deva's waves, with lightning glance,
Reflected to the day.
But who the torrent wave compels
A conqueror's chains to bear?
Let those who wake the soul that dwells
On our free winds, beware!
The greenest and the loveliest dells
May be the lion's lair!

Sung to the late-eighteenth-century tune of 'The Rising of the Lark' by Elizabeth Grant, the words were written by the English poet Felicia Hemans in the nineteenth century. The song is about Owain Glyndŵr's revolt against English rule in Wales in 1400. A descendent of the princes of Powys, Glyndŵr (or Glyndyr) soon controlled most of Wales. However, by 1408 he had been defeated by Prince Henry, later King Henry V.

CHARLIE IS MY DARLING

CHORUS:
Oh! Charlie is my darling, my darling, my darling!
Oh! Charlie is my darling, the young chevalier.

'Twas on a Monday morning,
Right early in the year,

When Charlie came to our town,
The young chevalier.

As he cam' marchin' up the street,
The pipes played loud and clear;
And a' the folk cam' rinnin' out,
To meet the chevalier.

CHORUS

Wi' Highland bonnets on their heads,
And claymores bright and clear,
They cam' to fight for Scotland's right,
And the young chevalier.

CHORUS

They've left their bonnie Highland hills,
Their wives and bairnies dear,
To draw the sword for Scotland's lord,
The young chevalier.

CHORUS

Oh! there were mony beating hearts,
And mony a hope and fear;
And mony were the pray'rs put up,
For the young chevalier.

CHORUS

This is a popular song celebrating the Jacobite rebellion of 1745 led by Prince Charles Edward Stuart, grandson of James II of England and VII of Scotland. Bonnie Prince Charlie was also known as the Young Pretender or Chevalier. He was finally defeated by King George II's forces at the Battle of Culloden in April 1746. The song has been attributed to the Scottish writer James Hogg and to Lady Carolina Nairne but both sometimes took existing traditional songs and adapted them. There is also a later version written by Robert Burns in 1794.

ᑌᘒ WHISKEY IN THE JAR ᘒᑌ

As I was going over the far famed Kerry mountains,
I met with Captain Farrell and his money he was
    counting.
I first produced my pistol, and then produced my rapier.
Said, 'Stand and deliver, for I am a bold deceiver!'

CHORUS:

Musha ring dum-a do dum-a da,
Whack for the daddy-o,
Whack for the daddy-o,
There's whiskey in the jar-o.

I counted out his money, and it made a pretty penny.
I put it in my pocket and I took it home to Jenny.
She said and she swore, that she never would deceive me,
But the devil take the women, for they never can be
    easy.

CHORUS

I went into my chamber, all for to take a slumber,
I dreamt of gold and jewels and for sure it was no wonder.
But Jenny took my charges and she filled them up with
    water,
Then sent for Captain Farrell to be ready for the
    slaughter.

CHORUS

It was early in the morning, as I rose up for travel,
The guards were all around me and likewise Captain
    Farrell,
I first produced my pistol, for she stole away my rapier,
But I couldn't shoot the water so a prisoner I was taken.

CHORUS

If anyone can aid me, it's my brother in the army,
If I can find his station down in Cork or in Killarney.
And if he'll come and save me, we'll go roving near
    Kilkenny,
And I swear he'll treat me better than me darling
    sportling Jenny.

CHORUS

Now some men take delight in the drinking and the roving,
But others take delight in the gambling and the
    smoking.
But I take delight in the juice of the barley,
And courting pretty fair maids in the morning bright
    and early.

CHORUS

This tale of a highwayman betrayed by his lover is a traditional Irish ballad set in the Mangerton mountains. It possibly dates back to the seventeenth century and the execution of a highwayman called Patrick Fleming around 1650. There are also suggestions that it inspired John Gay to write *The Beggar's Opera* in 1728. There are several American versions set in the US and it is very widely known, with slight variations in the lyrics, after being recorded by various folk and rock bands from the Dubliners and Pogues, to Thin Lizzy, Metallica and the Grateful Dead.

CHAPTER 6

It's Now We're Out to Sea My Boys: A Life on the Ocean Waves

A life spent at sea was a harsh one and songs of the sea tend to focus on the everyday realities and hardships of life for sailors and fishermen. Ports in the seventeenth and eighteenth centuries could be dangerous places where press gangs regularly recruited 'volunteers' to serve in the navy. Sea shanties were sailors' work songs sung to accompany certain tasks on board sailing ships and usually had a brisk, rhythmic pace to encourage efficiency. They declined with the development of clippers and more modern ships which needed smaller crews and different skills.

❧ BLOW YE WINDS BLOW ❧

'Tis advertised in Boston, New York, and Buffalo,
Five hundred brave Americans a-whaling for to go.

CHORUS:
> *Singing, blow ye winds in the morning,*
> *Blow ye winds, High-ho,*
> *Clear away your running gear*
> *And blow, blow, blow.*

They'll send you to New Bedford town, that famous
   whaling port,
And hand you to some land-sharks there to board and fit
   you out.

CHORUS

They tell you of the clipper ships, a-going in and out,
They say you'll take five hundred sperm before you're six
   months out.

CHORUS

It's now we're out to sea, my boys, the winds begin to
   blow,
One half the watch is sick on deck, the other half below.

CHORUS

Then comes the running rigging, which you're supposed
   to know,
It's 'Lay aloft, you sonofagun, or overboard you'll go.'

CHORUS

> The skipper's on the quarterdeck, a-squintin' at the sails,
> When up aloft the lookout sights a helluva school of
>   whales.

CHORUS

> 'So clear away the boots, me boys, and after them we'll
>   travel,
> But if you get too near his flukes, he'll kick you to the
>   devil.'

CHORUS

> Now we've got him turned up and towing alongside,
> We over with our blubberhooks and rob him of his hide.

CHORUS

> Next comes the stowing down, me lads, it takes both
>   night and day,
> And you'll all get fifty cents apiece on the 190th lay.

CHORUS

> And when the ship is full of oil and we don't give a
>   damn,
> We'll bend on all our stu'nsails and head for Yankeeland.

CHORUS

When we get home, our ship made fast, and we are
    through our sailing,
A winding glass around we'll pass and damn this
    blubber-whaling.

CHORUS

This American whaling ballad was traditionally sung to an older English tune. It describes an ordinary seaman's life on board a New England whaler. In the nineteenth century, New Bedford, Massachusetts, was one of the most important whaling ports in the world. The lyrics also show how many maritime terms have gradually been assimilated into everyday language. 'Son of a gun' originally meant 'bastard', dating from a time when it was common practice for women to go aboard ships in port. As most sailors slept in hammocks hung between the gun bulwarks, many babies were conceived literally under the guns.

WHAT SHALL WE DO WITH THE DRUNKEN SAILOR?

What shall we do with the drunken sailor?
What shall we do with the drunken sailor?
What shall we do with the drunken sailor?
Early in the morning!

CHORUS:

> *Weigh heigh and up she rises,*
> *Weigh heigh and up she rises,*
> *Weigh heigh and up she rises,*
> *Early in the morning!*

Put him in a long boat till he's sober, *(×3)*
Early in the morning!

CHORUS

Stick him in the scuppers with a hosepipe on him, *(×3)*
Early in the morning!

CHORUS

Shave his belly with a rusty razor, *(×3)*
Early in the morning!

CHORUS

Put him in bed with the captain's daughter, *(×3)*
Early in the morning!

CHORUS

That's what we do with a drunken sailor, *(×3)*
Early in the morning.

CHORUS ×2

ADDITIONAL VERSES THAT ARE SOMETIMES INCLUDED:

Put him in the long boat and make him bail her
Keep him there and make 'im bail 'er
Beat him with a cat 'til his back is bleedin'
Put him in the bilge and make him drink it

Pull out the bung and wet him all over
Truss him up with a running bowline
Heave him by the leg with a runnin' bowline
Give him a dose of salt and water
Stick on his back a mustard plaster
Give 'im a taste of the bosun's rope-end
Give 'im a hair of the dog that bit him
Send him to the crow's nest till he falls over
Tie him to the taffrail when she's yardarm under
Soak 'im in oil 'til he sprouts a flipper
Lock him in the guardroom 'til he's sober

Despite being one of the few sea shanties to be sung in the British Royal Navy, the first published reference to it is in an American account of a whaling ship sailing from New London, Connecticut, to the Pacific in 1839. The song is likely to be older than that, however, and British in origin. At the beginning of the nineteenth century, the poet and writer John Masefield described it as a 'walk away' shanty used for tacking, which would have been sung at a walking pace. It became more widely popular among the general public during the twentieth century.

Note: early is usually pronounced 'earl-aye'.

❦ MAID OF AMSTERDAM ❧

In Amsterdam there lived a maid,
Mark well what I do say,
In Amsterdam there lived a maid,

And she was mistress of her trade,
I'll go no more a-roving with you fair maid.

CHORUS:

A-roving, a-roving, since roving's been my ruin-o,
I'll go no more a-roving with you fair maid.

I took that fair maid for a walk,
Mark well what I do say,
I took that fair maid for a walk,
She said, 'Young man I'd rather talk,'
I'll go no more a-roving with you fair maid.

CHORUS

I put my hand upon her thigh,
Mark well what I do say,
I put my hand upon her thigh,
She said, 'Young man you're rather high!'
I'll go no more a-roving with you fair maid.

CHORUS

Her lovely arms were white as milk,
Mark well what I do say,
Her lovely arms were white as milk,
Her flaxen hair was soft as silk,
I'll go no more a-roving with you fair maid.

CHORUS

But when I got back home from sea,
Mark well what I do say,
When I got back home from sea,

A soldier had her on his knee,
I'll go no more a-roving with you fair maid.

CHORUS

This is a capstan or pump shanty sung to match the downward movement of the pump wheel, vitally pumping out the water that leaked into the ship. There are French, Flemish, Dutch and Danish versions of the song which may date back to the Elizabethan age. The earliest printed record of the shanty is in *The Rape of Lucrece*, Thomas Heywood's play of 1608.

❧ SPANISH LADIES ❧

Farewell and adieu to you fair Spanish ladies,
Farewell and adieu to you ladies of Spain,
For we've received orders for to sail for old England,
But we hope in a short while to see you again.

CHORUS:
We'll rant and we'll roar like true British sailors,
We'll rant and we'll roar across the wide sea,
Until we strike soundings in the channel of old England,
From the Ushant to the Scillies is thirty-five leagues.

Now we hove our ship to with the wind at sou'west,
    boys,
We hove our ship to for to make soundings clear,

We had forty-five fathom and a fine sandy bottom,
So we filled the main topsail and up channel steered.

CHORUS

Now the first land we met it is known as the Dead Man,
Next Ramhead off Plymouth, Start, Portland and Wight,
For we sailed past Beachy passed Fairlee to Dungeness,
Then we bore her away for the South Foreland light.

CHORUS

Now the signal was made for the grand fleet to anchor,
All day in the Downs that night for to moor,
Stand by your shank painter, let fly your cat stopper,
Haul up your clew garnets, stick out tacks and sheets.

CHORUS

Now let every man swig off a full bumper,
Now let every man swig off a full bowl,
So drink and be merry, drive away melancholy,
For we'll drink to each jovial good-hearted soul.

CHORUS

'Spanish Ladies' was originally a British naval song told from the viewpoint of the crew looking out for landmarks on the voyage home from Spain. A ballad of the same name was registered by the English Stationer's Company in 1624 and the song is mentioned in HMS *Nellie*'s logbook of 1796. It is also sometimes described as a capstan shanty, sung by sailors as they raised anchor.

❦ OH, SHENANDOAH ❧

Oh, Shenandoah,
I long to hear you,
Away you rolling river,
Oh, Shenandoah,
I long to hear you,
Away, I'm bound away
'Cross the wide Missouri.

Oh, Shenandoah,
I love your daughter,
Away you rolling river,
I'll take her 'cross
Your rollin' water,
Away, I'm bound away
'Cross the wide Missouri.

'Tis seven years,
I've been a rover,
Away you rolling river,
When I return,
I'll be your lover,
Away, I'm bound away
'Cross the wide Missouri.

Oh, Shenandoah,
I'm bound to leave you,
Away you rolling river,
Oh, Shenandoah,

I'll not deceive you,
Away, I'm bound away
'Cross the wide Missouri.

'Oh, Shenandoah' is said to have originated with French voyageurs, the fur trappers and traders who regularly sailed along the Missouri river in the early nineteenth century, though it has also been claimed by the US cavalry who fought against the Native Americans in the region. The song tells the story of a sailor who fell in love with the daughter of Shenandoah, chief of the Oneida Iroquois. In the nineteenth century the song became popular as a capstan shanty sung by British as well as American crews sailing out of New Orleans.

WHEN THE BOAT COMES IN

Come here, maw little Jacky,
Now aw've smoked mi backy,
Let's hev a bit o'cracky,
Till the boat comes in.

Dance ti' thy daddy, sing ti' thy mammy,
Dance ti' thy daddy, ti' thy mammy sing;
Thou shall hev a fishy on a little dishy,
Thou shall hev a fishy when the boat comes in.

Here's thy mother humming,
Like a canny woman;

Yonder comes thy father,
Drunk – he cannot stand.

Dance ti' thy daddy, sing ti' thy mammy,
Dance ti' thy daddy, ti' thy mammy sing;
Thou shall hev a fishy on a little dishy,
Thou shall hev a haddock when the boat comes in.

Our Tommy's always fuddling,
He's so fond of ale,
But he's kind to me,
I hope he'll never fail.

Dance ti' thy daddy, sing ti' thy mammy,
Dance ti' thy daddy, ti' thy mammy sing;
Thou shall hev a fishy on a little dishy,
Thou shall hev a bloater when the boat comes in.

I like a drop mysel',
When I can get it sly,
And thou, my bonny bairn,
Will lik't as well as I.

Dance ti' thy daddy, sing ti' thy mammy,
Dance ti' thy daddy, ti' thy mammy sing;
Thou shall hev a fishy on a little dishy,
Thou shall hev a mackerel when the boat comes in.

May we get a drop,
Oft as we stand in need;
And weel may the keel row
That brings the bairns their bread.

> Dance ti' thy daddy, sing ti' thy mammy,
> Dance ti' thy daddy, ti' thy mammy sing;
> Thou shall hev a fishy on a little dishy,
> Thou shall hev a salmon when the boat comes in.

This is a popular Northumbrian folk song where the family awaits the fisherman father's return. There are some variations in the title and wording, but this is the version used in the 1970s BBC drama series of the same name. The song appeared in an early Newcastle broadside and was published in a collection of ballads from Northern England by William Watson at the beginning of the nineteenth century. It was also included in one of Cecil Sharp's compilations.

❧ BLOW THE WIND SOUTHERLY ☙

> Blow the wind Southerly, Southerly, Southerly,
> Blow the wind South o'er the bonnie blue sea;
> Blow the wind Southerly, Southerly, Southerly,
> Blow bonnie breeze, my true lover to me.
>
> They told me last night there were ships in the offing,
> And I hurried down to the deep rolling sea;
> But my eye could not see it wherever might be it,
> The bark that is bearing my lover to me.

Blow the wind Southerly, Southerly, Southerly,
Blow bonnie breeze o'er the bonnie blue sea;
Blow the wind Southerly, Southerly, Southerly,
Blow bonnie breeze, and bring him to me.

Oh, is it not sweet to hear the breeze singing,
As lightly it comes o'er the deep rolling sea?
But sweeter and dearer by far when 'tis bringing,
The bark of my true love in safety to me.

This is another well-known Northumbrian folk song from
Tyneside. The first two verses were printed in *The Bishoprick
Garland* of 1834, a collection of cultural practices from the
Bishopric of Durham, but they are thought to be just a fragment
of a longer ballad. The theme of a woman left behind at home
awaiting the safe return of a lover from sea is a very common one.

THE LORELEI

I know not if there is a reason
Why I am so sad at heart.
A legend of bygone ages
Haunts me and will not depart.

The air is cool under nightfall.
The calm Rhine courses its way.
The peak of the mountain is sparkling
With evening's final ray.

The fairest of maidens is sitting
So marvellous up there,
Her golden jewels are shining,
She's combing her golden hair.

She combs with a comb also golden,
And sings a song as well,
Whose melody binds a wondrous
And overpowering spell.

In his little boat, the boatman
Is seized with a savage woe,
He'd rather look up at the mountain
Than down at the rocks below.

I think that the waves will devour
The boatman and boat as one;
And this by her song's sheer power
Fair Lorelei has done.

The Lorelei is a rock that soars high above a narrow stretch of the River Rhine where strong currents and hidden rocks make the area notoriously hazardous for sailors. A legend grew up of a mermaid or siren who lived there and lured sailors to their deaths with her beauty and singing. The German writer Heinrich Heine wrote the original poem, published in 1827, which was then set to music by Friedrich Silcher, becoming one of Germany's most famous folk songs. This English translation is by A. Z. Foreman.

✺ THE BAY OF BISCAY ✺

Loud roar'd the dreadful thunder,
The rain a deluge show'rs,
The clouds were rent asunder
By lighting's vivid pow'rs.
The night was drear and dark,
Our poor devoted bark,
Till next day there she lay
In the Bay of Biscay, O!

Now, dash'd upon the billow,
Her op'ning timbers creak,
Each fears a wat'ry pillow,
None stop the dreadful leak.
To cling to slipp'ry shrouds,
Each breathless seaman crowds,
As she lay till next day
In the Bay of Biscay, O!

At length the wish'd for morrow
Broke thro' the hazy sky,
Absorb'd in silent sorrow,
Each heav'd a bitter sigh,
The dismal wreck to view,
Struck horror in the crew,
As she lay all that day
In the Bay of Biscay, O!

Her yielding timbers sever,
Her pitchy seams are rent,

> When Heav'n, all bounteous ever,
> It's boundless mercy sent,
> A sail in sight appears,
> We hail her with three cheers,
> Now we sail, with the gale,
> From the Bay of Biscay, O!

A great number of songs were inspired by the Bay of Biscay, off the western coast of France, infamous for its treacherous currents and devastating storms. Many sailors perished there. In this song written by Andrew Cherry at the beginning of the nineteenth century there is, however, a happy ending. Cherry was an actor and writer for the stage, leaving his father's printing and bookselling company in Dublin for London's Drury Lane.

CHAPTER 7

I'll Tell Me Ma: Children's Songs & Rhymes

Songs traditionally sung by children are among the most enduring and well remembered. Sometimes used as the accompaniment to playground games or cautionary tales, these rhymes have a long history. Many have links back to the Georgians or even the Elizabethans; a few are truly ancient. Most are deceptively simple, their lyrics surprisingly dark, reflecting past events and characters that have long been forgotten.

❦ LONDON BRIDGE ❧
IS FALLING DOWN

London Bridge is falling down,
Falling down, falling down,
London Bridge is falling down,
My fair lady.

Build it up with wood and clay,
Wood and clay, wood and clay,
Build it up with wood and clay,
My fair lady.

Wood and clay will wash away,
Wash away, wash away,
Wood and clay will wash away,
My fair lady.

Build it up with bricks and mortar,
Bricks and mortar, bricks and mortar,
Build it up with bricks and mortar,
My fair lady.

Bricks and mortar will not stay,
Will not stay, will not stay,
Bricks and mortar will not stay,
My fair lady.

Build it up with iron and steel,
Iron and steel, iron and steel,

Build it up with iron and steel,
My fair lady.

Iron and steel will bend and bow,
Bend and bow, bend and bow,
Iron and steel will bend and bow,
My fair lady.

Build it up with silver and gold,
Silver and gold, silver and gold,
Build it up with silver and gold,
My fair lady.

Silver and gold will be stolen away,
Stolen away, stolen away,
Silver and gold will be stolen away,
My fair lady.

Set a man to watch all night,
Watch all night, watch all night,
Set a man to watch all night,
My fair lady.

Suppose the man should fall asleep,
Fall asleep, fall asleep,
Suppose the man should fall asleep,
My fair lady.

Give him a pipe to smoke all night,
Smoke all night, smoke all night,
Give him a pipe to smoke all night,
My fair lady.

The first verse in particular is very well known and the rhyme has a long history. The earliest printed version appeared around 1744 when the first line was 'London Bridge is broken down'. There are various theories about the rhyme's origins, the simplest being that it reflected the number of different London Bridges that have existed over the centuries, the first being a simple military pontoon constructed by the Romans.

However, versions of the rhyme are known across Europe dating back to the fourteenth century at least. There is also a game associated with it where two players form a bridge while everyone else passes underneath holding onto the person in front, hoping not to be the one caught when the bridge falls. It may be that the rhyme simply adopted London Bridge as the most famous bridge in England and that its origins lie further back in antiquity. The mention of a watchman also echoes superstitions that malevolent water spirits must be appeased for a bridge to stand firm, hence ancient rites where people, often children, were walled into foundations to act as guardian spirits – sometimes when still alive. Reassuringly, there is no archaeological evidence of any human remains in the foundations of London Bridge.

RING-A-RING O' ROSES

> Ring-a-ring o' roses
> A pocket full of posies,
> Atishoo! Atishoo!
> We all fall down.
>
> The cows are in the meadow,
> Lying fast asleep,
> Atishoo! Atishoo!
> We all get up.

We've all heard the story that this children's song is really about the Great Plague of 1665–6 but the truth is a little less exciting. The version of the rhyme we sing today seems to have appeared in the nineteenth century and is similar to other songs known throughout Europe that involve games played during dances. A Massachusetts ditty with the same tune was recorded a little earlier in 1790:

> Ring-a-ring-a rosie,
> A bottle full of posie,

All the girls in our town,
Ring for little Josie.

MARY, MARY, QUITE CONTRARY

Mary, Mary, quite contrary,
How does your garden grow?
With silver bells and cockle shells,
And pretty maids all in a row.

The origins of this simple song are hotly debated with many theories and little evidence. Most look back to the religious upheaval of Tudor times. The rhyme has been seen as an allegory of the Catholic Church with the bells representing the *sanctus* bells, the cockle shells the badges worn by pilgrims, and the pretty maids being the nuns. Whether it is mourning the persecution of the Catholic Church by Henry VIII and Elizabeth I, or its reinstatement under Mary Tudor is not clear. Traditionally 'Mary' is thought to be Mary Queen of Scots, although she could also be Mary Tudor – 'quite contrary' because she reversed the religious changes of her father Henry VIII and brother Edward VI, and the 'silver bells and cockle shells' could have been instruments of torture to be used against heretics. The rhyme first appeared in print around 1744.

THE GRAND OLD DUKE OF YORK

Oh the grand old Duke of York,
He had ten thousand men,
He marched them up to the top of the hill,
And he marched them down again.

And when they were up, they were up,
And when they were down, they were down,
And when they were only halfway up,
They were neither up nor down.

The oldest recorded version of the song dates from 1642 with the opening line, 'The King of France with forty thousand men', and over the years it has also been sung about Napoleon. As the rhyme seems to refer to a specific historical character there has been great speculation about the identity of the Duke. One possibility is that he could be Richard of York, killed at the Battle of Wakefield in 1460 while waiting for reinforcements at the hill-top Sandal Castle. Unpopular King James II, also Duke of York, is another candidate. He marched his army to Salisbury Plain to resist the invasion by his son-in-law William III, only to retreat without fighting. The character most often suggested is Prince Frederick, Duke of York, and second son of George III. He was commander-in-chief of British troops during the Napoleonic Wars and, following a defeat in the Flanders Campaign, he was recalled to London. Though Flanders is generally flat, the town of Cassel is built on a small hill.

I'LL TELL ME MA

I'll tell me Ma when I go home
The boys won't leave the girls alone
They pull my hair, they stole my comb
But that's alright till I go home.

She is handsome, she is pretty
She is the belle of Belfast city
She is courtin' one, two, three
Please won't you tell me, who is she?

Albert Mooney says he loves her
All the boys are fighting for her
They knock at the door and they ring that bell
'Oh my true love, are you well?'
Out she comes as white as snow
Rings on her fingers and bells on her toes
Old Jenny Marray says she will die
If she doesn't get the fellow
With the roving eye.

I'll tell me Ma when I go home
The boys won't leave the girls alone
They pull my hair, they stole my comb
But that's alright till I go home.

She is handsome, she is pretty
She is the belle of Belfast city
She is courtin' one, two, three
Please won't you tell me, who is she?

Let the wind and the rain and the hail blow high
And the snow come tumbling from the sky
She's as nice as apple pie
She'll get her own lad by and by
When she gets a lad of her own
She won't tell her Ma when she comes home
Let them all come as they will
For it's Albert Mooney she loves still.

I'll tell me Ma when I go home
The boys won't leave the girls alone
They pull my hair, they stole my comb
But that's alright till I go home.

She is handsome, she is pretty
She is the belle of Belfast city
She is courtin' one, two, three
Please won't you tell me, who is she?

The song has been recorded by various popular artists including Van Morrison, the Chieftains and the Dubliners. Popularly associated with Belfast, 'I'll Tell Me Ma' was well known throughout England and Ireland in the nineteenth century. Although the theme is the perennial one of who likes whom, it was a children's song, sung to accompany a traditional game where children hold hands and form a circle, with one player in the centre.

GET ALONG HOME, CINDY

Cindy is a pretty girl,
She comes from the South,
She's so sweet the honey-bees
Swarm around her mouth.

CHORUS:
Get along home,
Get along home,
Get along home, Cindy, Cindy,
I'll marry you some day.

She told me that she loved me,
She called me sugar-plum,

She flang her arms around me
And I thought my time had come.

CHORUS

Cindy were to the meetin',
She shouted and she sung,
She got so full of glory
She shook her stockings down.

CHORUS

Cindy got religion,
She'd had it once before,
But when she heard my old banjo,
She was the first one on the floor.

CHORUS

Preacher in the pulpit
Preachin' mighty bold,
Preachin' for the money
To save the sinner's soul.

CHORUS

I went down to Cindy's house,
Cindy wasn't home,
I set down in Cindy's chair
And rocked until she come.

CHORUS

I went to see my Cindy,
Carried a pair of shoes,
Asked her if she'd marry me,
She said she couldn't refuse.

CHORUS

> I wish I had a needle,
> As fine as I could sew,
> I'd sew that gal to my coat-tail
> And down the road I'd go.

CHORUS

This is a traditional American children's song that was first recorded in Kentucky in 1933. It seems to have developed from a blackface minstrel song called 'Cindy Lou' but was popular with Southern mountain musicians as a dance reel. Extra verses were added and it would have been sung along to a banjo or fiddle, combining old British and American rhythms.

SHE'LL BE COMING ROUND THE MOUNTAIN WHEN SHE COMES

She'll be coming round the mountain when she
    comes,
She'll be coming round the mountain when she
    comes,
She'll be coming round the mountain, coming round
    the mountain,
She'll be coming round the mountain when she
    comes.

She'll be driving six white horses when she comes,
She'll be driving six white horses when she comes,
She'll be driving six white horses, driving six white horses,
She'll be driving six white horses when she comes.

Oh, we'll all go out to meet her when she comes,
Oh, we'll all go out to meet her when she comes,
Oh, we'll all go out to meet her, all go out to meet her,
Oh, we'll all go out to meet her when she comes.

She'll be carrying three white puppies when she comes,
She'll be carrying three white puppies when she comes,
She'll be carrying three white puppies, carrying three
      white puppies,
She'll be carrying three white puppies when she comes.

We will kill the old red rooster when she comes,
We will kill the old red rooster when she comes,
We will kill the old red rooster, kill the old red rooster,
We will kill the old red rooster when she comes.

We will all have chicken and dumplings when she comes,
We will all have chicken and dumplings when she comes,
We will all have chicken and dumplings, all have chicken
      and dumplings,
We will all have chicken and dumplings when she comes.

We'll be shouting Hallelujah when she comes,
We'll be shouting Hallelujah when she comes,
We'll be shouting Hallelujah, shouting Hallelujah,
We'll be shouting Hallelujah when she comes.

Now usually considered a children's song, this rather jolly uptempo piece was first published in *The American Songbook* of 1927 by the multiple Pulitzer Prize winner Carl Sandburg. It is thought to date from the early nineteenth century and an old spiritual song called 'When the Chariot Comes'. As it spread throughout the Appalachians the lyrics were changed and by the 1890s it was popular with Midwestern railroad workers.

FIRE'S BURNING

Fire's burning, fire's burning,
Draw nearer, draw nearer,
In the gloaming, in the gloaming,
Come sing and be merry.

Usually sung as a two-part round, 'Fire's Burning' was popular with scouts and girl guides from the 1940s onwards. It is one of the best-known campfire songs using the same tune as 'London's Burning'.

❧ GING GANG GOOLIE ❧

Ging gang goolie goolie goolie goolie watcha,
Ging gang goo, ging gang goo.
Ging gang goolie goolie goolie goolie watcha,
Ging gang goo, ging gang goo.
Hayla, hayla shayla, hayla shayla, shayla, oh-ho,
Hayla, hayla shayla, hayla shayla, shayla, oh.
Shally wally, shally wally, shally wally, shally wally,
Oompah, oompah, oompah, oompah.

Another favourite campfire song, usually sung as a round. It was first made popular among the scouts by the organization's founder Robert Baden-Powell, most likely during the First World Scout Jamboree of 1920. The idea was that children worldwide could all sing these nonsense lyrics irrespective of the language they spoke.

❧ MY SHIP SAILED ❧
FROM CHINA

My ship sailed from China,
With a cargo of tea,
All laden with goodies for you and for me.
They brought me a fan,
Just imagine my bliss,

When I fan myself daily,
Like this, like this, like this, like this.

My ship sailed from China,
They brought me a brush,
Just imagine my bliss,
When I brush my hair briskly,
Like this, like this, like this, like this.

My ship sailed from China,
They brought me some shoes,
Just imagine my bliss,
When I tap my feet lightly,
Like this, like this, like this, like this.

AND SO ON UNTIL THE FINAL VERSE

My ship crashed in China,
With a cargo of tea,
All laden with goodies for you and for me.
I didn't get my fan,
Just imagine my bliss,
I can stop fanning myself,
Like this, like this, like this, like this.

Sung by generations around the campfire with movement and actions. There are few fixed verses as part of the fun was making up new lines. As with most of these campfire songs, the origins are obscure. They are classic sing-along tunes, passed on by word of mouth, and seem to have grown out of the enjoyment of camping out with friends.

CHAPTER 8

Green Grow the Rushes, O: A Wing & a Prayer

For centuries, most people from Christian countries would have been involved in some form of religious singing on a weekly basis at church, chapel and school. There are many songs with religious themes, some with obscure origins that seem to draw on older legends. In the nineteenth century, while it was common for evangelical leaders to strongly discourage any non-religious singing, it is likely that secular and Christian songs were sometimes combined. This was also true of the early Puritan settlers in the New World and a great number of early American folk songs were religious. Plantation slaves added their own rhythms and a strong tradition of spiritual singing developed among slave communities.

AMAZING GRACE

Amazing grace, how sweet the sound
That saved a wretch like me.
I once was lost, but now am found,
Was blind, but now I see.

'Twas grace that taught my heart to fear,
And grace my fears relieved;
How precious did that grace appear
The hour I first believed.

Through many dangers, toils and snares,
I have already come;
'Tis grace has brought me safe thus far,
And grace will lead me home.

The Lord has promised good to me,
His Word my hope secures;
He will my shield and portion be,
As long as life endures.

Yea, when this flesh and heart shall fail,
And mortal life shall cease,
I shall possess, within the veil,
A life of joy and peace.

The earth shall soon dissolve like snow,
The sun forbear to shine;
But God, who called me here below,
Will be forever mine.

When we've been there ten thousand years
Bright shining as the sun,
We've no less days to sing God's praise
Than when we've first begun.

Famously written by John Newton and published in 1779, the first verse was inspired by Newton's conversion to evangelical Christianity in 1748 at the age of twenty-three, after a night on board a storm-lashed ship, facing the prospect of drowning. Before this traumatic event, Newton had already experienced a long career on the seas, having first set sail with his father at the age of eleven and then spending some years as a dissolute adventurer. Flogged as a naval deserter, he worked for a slave trader in Africa where he was starved and ill-treated. Newton went on to command a slave ship until he ended his seafaring to study theology. He was ordained as a curate in 1764 and began writing hymns with William Cowper. 'Amazing Grace' may have originally been written for a sermon in 1773.

HE'S GOT THE WHOLE WORLD IN HIS HANDS

He's got the whole world in His hands,
He's got the whole wide world in His hands,
He's got the whole world in His hands,
He's got the whole world in His hands.

He's got the wind and the rain in His hands, *(×3)*
He's got the whole world in His hands.

He's got the little tiny baby in His hands, *(×3)*
He's got the whole world in His hands.

He's got you and me, brother, in His hands, *(×3)*
He's got the whole world in His hands.

He's got you and me, sister, in His hands, *(×3)*
He's got the whole world in His hands.

He's got ev'rybody here in His hands, *(×3)*
He's got the whole world in His hands.

This well-known American spiritual was published in 1927 in *Spirituals Triumphant, Old and New* but is likely to be much older. It seems to have been widely sung in various US states including North Carolina and Alabama. These are the verses most usually included but there are many others, including some more innovative ones: 'He's got the back-sliding sister in His hands' and 'the crap-shooting man'.

❦ SWING LOW, SWEET CHARIOT ❧

CHORUS:
Swing low, sweet chariot,
Coming for to carry me home,

Swing low, sweet chariot,
Coming for to carry me home.

I looked over Jordan, and what did I see,
Coming for to carry me home?
A band of angels coming after me,
Coming for to carry me home.

CHORUS

Sometimes I'm up, and sometimes I'm down,
Coming for to carry me home,
But still my soul feels heavenly bound,
Coming for to carry me home.

CHORUS

The brightest day that I can say,
Coming for to carry me home,
When Jesus washed my sins away,
Coming for to carry me home.

CHORUS

If you get there before I do,
Coming for to carry me home,
Tell all my friends I'm coming there too,
Coming for to carry me home.

CHORUS

Now famously sung by rugby fans, 'Swing Low' has been the England rugby team's anthem since the early 1990s. The American spiritual was first recorded in 1909 by the Fisk University Jubilee Singers, in Nashville, Tennessee, but it was written earlier, around the middle of the nineteenth century, by Wallis Willis from Choctaw County, Oklahoma. There are suggestions that this and 'Steal Away', another of Willis' songs, contain references to the Underground Railroad which helped Southern slaves escape to freedom in the North and Canada. The original Fisk Singers performed along the route of the Underground Railroad.

KUMBAYA

Kumbaya, my Lord, kumbaya,
Kumbaya, my Lord, kumbaya,
Kumbaya, my Lord, kumbaya,
Oh Lord, kumbaya.

Someone's singing, my Lord, kumbaya, *(×3)*
Oh Lord, kumbaya.

Someone's laughing, my Lord, kumbaya, *(×3)*
Oh Lord, kumbaya.

Someone's crying, my Lord, kumbaya, *(×3)*
Oh Lord, kumbaya.

Someone's praying, my Lord, kumbaya, *(×3)*
Oh Lord, kumbaya.

Someone's sleeping, my Lord, kumbaya, *(×3)*
Oh Lord, kumbaya.

Another American spiritual first recorded in the 1920s. The word 'kumbaya' may be a derivation of the song 'Come by Yuh' from South Carolina, sung in Gullah, the Creole language, or it may come from 'Come by Here' also a traditional spiritual of the time. The song was popularized during the folk revival of the 1950s and 1960s.

GREEN GROW THE RUSHES

I'll sing you one, O
Green grow the rushes, O
What is your one, O?
One is one and all alone
And evermore shall be so.

I'll sing you two, O
Green grow the rushes, O
What are your two, O?
Two, two, lily-white boys,
Clothed all in green, O
One is one and all alone
And evermore shall be so.

I'll sing you three, O
Green grow the rushes, O
What are your three, O?
Three, three, the rivals,
Two, two, lily-white boys,
Clothed all in green, O
One is one and all alone
And evermore shall be so.

AND SO ON, WITH EACH NEW VERSE
ADDING ADDITIONAL LINES:

Four for the Gospel makers,
Five for the symbols at your door,
Six for the six proud walkers,
Seven for the seven stars in the sky,
Eight for the eight bold rangers,
Nine for the nine bright shiners,
Ten for the ten commandments,
Eleven for the eleven who went to heaven,

FINAL VERSE:

I'll sing you twelve, O
Green grow the rushes, O
What are your twelve, O?
Twelve for the twelve Apostles,
Eleven for the eleven who went to heaven,
Ten for the ten commandments,
Nine for the nine bright shiners,
Eight for the eight bold rangers,
Seven for the seven stars in the sky,
Six for the six proud walkers,
Five for the symbols at your door,

Four for the Gospel makers,
Three, three, the rivals,
Two, two, lily-white boys,
Clothed all in green, O
One is one and all alone
And evermore shall be so.

At one time known as the 'Dilly Song', 'Green Grow the Rushes' has ancient and mysterious origins. There are versions in most European languages, including medieval Latin. At one time the song may have been used to teach the Creed with two verses added to the earlier ten to match the twelve Apostles. The wording has changed over time and any pre-Christian references have been lost. The meaning of many of the lines is obscure to say the least.

One is usually taken to mean God, while the two lily-white boys or maids are thought to be Christ and John the Baptist, dating from a time when a 'maid' could be male or female. The three rivals are often said to be the Wise Men, while the symbol at your door may be the pentagram. The six proud walkers are commonly believed to represent the water jars from the Gospel account of the wedding at Cana, and the seven stars are from the constellation *Ursa Major*, or the Great Bear. Eight bold rangers, sometimes called April rainers, may refer to angels, while nine bright shiners, or gable rangers, could be a reference to the Archangel Gabriel.

The song is sometimes included with Christmas carols and has also been sung at Easter passion plays.

❧ A MAY DAY CAROL ❧

The moon shines bright and the stars give a light,
A little before 'tis day;
Our Lord our God, He called to us,
And bid us awake and pray.

Awake, awake, oh pretty, pretty maid,
Out of your drowsy dream;
And step into your dairy below,
And fetch me a bowl of cream.

If not a bowl of thy sweet cream,
A cup to bring me cheer;
For the Lord knows when we shall meet again,
To go Maying another year.

I have been wandering all this night,
And some time of this day;
And now returning home again,
I've brought you a branch of May.

A branch of May I've brought you here,
And at your door I stand;
'Tis nothing but a sprout, but well budded out,
By the work of our Lord's hand.

My song is done and I must be gone,
No longer can I stay;
So it's God bless you all, both great and small,
And send you a joyful May.

Also known as 'The Moon Shines Bright', this folk-carol was popular with carollers at May Day and Christmas when it was sung with alternate verses to match the time of year. It appeared regularly in broadsides from the late eighteenth century. This version refers to a budding branch of May, which would have been carried from door to door for good luck just as a wassail bough would have been at Christmastime.

CHAPTER 9

For the Sake of Auld Lang Syne: At the Year's End

In the Victorian age, a strong tradition developed in Britain and Ireland for groups of village musicians to sing carols at Christmas and occasionally Easter, as well as other notable times of the year. They would walk the streets, stopping at houses and the local pub. Many new carols were written in the nineteenth century but the carollers' repertoire would always include a number of folk-carols. Some of these dated back to Elizabethan and even earlier medieval times when carols were usually sung by travelling minstrels, and in the home rather than church. Oliver Cromwell put a stop to this when he came to power in 1649 but people continued to sing in secret. In 1915, the folk-music scholars Frank Kidson and Mary Neal wrote that several of the carols published by Cecil Sharp and Ralph Vaughan Williams 'embody curious legends, the origin of which is difficult to trace'.

Joseph was an old man
And an old man was he
And Joseph married Mary
The Queen of Galilee.

Mary and Joseph
Together did go
And there they saw a cherry tree
Both red, white and green.

Then up speaks Mary
So meek and so mild,
'Oh gather me cherries, Joseph
For I am with child.'

Then up speaks Joseph
With his words so unkind,
'Let them gather thee cherries
That brought thee with child.'

Then up speaks the little child
In his own mother's womb,
'Bow down, you sweet cherry tree
And give my mother some.'

Then the top spray of the cherry tree
Bowed down to her knee,
'And now you see, Joseph
There are cherries for me.'

This is often said to be just one part of a longer ballad dating from the Middle Ages, although no other sections have ever been found. It seems to draw on the Biblical story of Mary and the fig tree from the Apocrypha, which was popular in England in the fourteenth century, with the native cherry tree replacing the fig. The song itself only appears in broadsides towards the end of the eighteenth century.

HERE WE COME A-WASSAILING

Here we come a-wassailing
Among the leaves so green,
Here we come a-wand'ring
So fairly to be seen.

CHORUS:
Love and joy come to you,
And to you our wassail, too,
And God bless you and send you
A Happy New Year,
God send you a Happy New Year.

Our wassail cup is made
Of the rosemary tree,
And so is your beer
Of the best barley.

CHORUS

We are not daily beggars
That beg from door to door,
But we are neighbours' children
That you have seen before.

Call up the butler of this house,
Put on his golden ring,
Let him bring us up a glass of beer,
And better shall we sing.

I have a little purse
It's made of leather skin,
I need a silver sixpence
To line it well within.

Bring us out a table,
And spread it with a cloth,
Bring us out a mouldy cheese
And some of your Christmas loaf.

God bless the master of this house,
Likewise the mistress, too,
And all the little children
That 'round the table grew.

Good master and good mistress,
While you're sitting by the fire,

Pray think of us poor children
Who are wandering in the mire.

CHORUS

Here we come a-wassailing
Among the leaves so green,
Here we come a-wand'ring
So fairly to be seen.

CHORUS

Often sung at New Year rather than Christmas, this carol was written down around 1850 but the tradition of wassailing, singing from door to door to wish good luck, dates back to the twelfth century. 'Wassail' is an old English toast to wish good health and it also refers to the hot spiced ale, or wine, that would be poured into the wassail cup or bowl. As in the 'May Day Carol', wassailers would sometimes take a bough or garland with them.

THE HOLLY
AND THE IVY

The holly and the ivy,
When they are both full grown,
Of all the trees that are in the wood,
The holly bears the crown.

CHORUS:

> *O, the rising of the sun,*
> *And the running of the deer,*
> *The playing of the merry organ,*
> *Sweet singing in the choir.*

The holly bears a berry,
As red as any blood,
And Mary bore sweet Jesus Christ,
To do poor sinners good.

CHORUS

The holly bears a blossom,
As white as lily flower,
And Mary bore sweet Jesus Christ,
To be our sweet Saviour.

CHORUS

The holly bears a bark,
As bitter as any gall,
And Mary bore sweet Jesus Christ,
For to redeem us all.

CHORUS

The holly bears a prickle,
As sharp as any thorn,
And Mary bore sweet Jesus Christ,
On Christmas Day in the morn.

CHORUS

O the holly bears a flower,
As white as any milk,

And Mary bore sweet Jesus Christ,
All wrapped up in silk.

CHORUS

The holly and the ivy,
When they are both full grown,
Of all the trees that are in the wood,
The holly bears the crown.

CHORUS

Using evergreens including holly and ivy to decorate houses and churches at Christmas and the close of the year is an ancient custom and relic of paganism. The earliest printed references to this carol are in a broadside of the early eighteenth century but it may be far older. The theme of rivalry between the holly and ivy is medieval with holly representing the masculine and ivy the feminine. Chaucer also calls the organ 'merry' in *The Nun's Priest's Tale*, whereas more modern writers tend to focus their descriptions on the instrument's strength or power.

❧ I SAW THREE SHIPS ❧

I saw three ships come sailing in,
On Christmas day, on Christmas day,
I saw three ships come sailing in,
On Christmas day in the morning.

And what was in those ships all three?
On Christmas day, on Christmas day,
And what was in those ships all three?
On Christmas day in the morning.

Our Saviour Christ and his lady,
On Christmas day, on Christmas day,
Our Saviour Christ and his lady,
On Christmas day in the morning.

Pray whither sailed those ships all three?
On Christmas day, on Christmas day,
Pray whither sailed those ships all three?
On Christmas day in the morning.

Oh, they sailed into Bethlehem,
On Christmas day, on Christmas day,
Oh, they sailed into Bethlehem,
On Christmas day in the morning.

And all the bells on earth shall ring,
On Christmas day, on Christmas day,
And all the bells on earth shall ring,
On Christmas day in the morning.

And all the Angels in Heaven shall sing,
On Christmas day, on Christmas day,
And all the Angels in Heaven shall sing,
On Christmas day in the morning.

And all the souls on earth shall sing,
On Christmas day, on Christmas day,

And all the souls on earth shall sing,
On Christmas day in the morning.

Then let us all rejoice again,
On Christmas day, on Christmas day,
Then let us all rejoice again,
On Christmas day in the morning.

Sung to the tune of a traditional English folk song, 'I Saw Three Ships' was probably composed by wandering minstrels in the later Middle Ages. Legend has it that three ships transported the skulls of the Wise Men to Cologne Cathedral in the twelfth century. Over the centuries the lyrics have changed to include different characters. This is the version most often remembered today.

HOLMFIRTH ANTHEM

Abroad for pleasure as I was a-walking,
It was one summer, summer evening clear,
There I beheld the most beautiful damsel,
Lamenting for her shepherd swain,
Lamenting for her shepherd swain.

The fairest evening that e'er I beheld,
Was ever, ever more with the lad I adore,
Wilt thou fight yon French and Spaniards,
Wilt thou leave me thus my dear,
Wilt thou leave me thus my dear.

No more to yon green banks will I take thee,
With pleasure for to rest yourself and view the land,
But I will take thee to yon green gardens,
Where the pratty flowers grow,
Where the pratty, pratty flowers grow.

I will take thee to yon green gardens,
Where the pratty flowers grow,
Where the pratty, pratty flowers grow.

Although not at all religious or even seasonal in content, this became a popular folk-carol and a staple for Yorkshire carollers to sing. It was originally called 'A Maiden's Complaint for the Loss of Her Shepherd' and was adapted by Joe Perkins, a choirmaster from Holmfirth in West Yorkshire, in 1850. Related folk songs have been recorded in other parts of England but they are very rare. As well as Christmas and the New Year, the song was often sung at Whitsun and village hunt meets.

❧ AULD LANG SYNE ☙

Should auld acquaintance be forgot,
And never brought to mind?
Should auld acquaintance be forgot,
And auld lang syne?

CHORUS:
And for auld lang syne, my jo,
For auld lang syne,

We'll tak a cup o' kindness yet,
For auld lang syne.

And surely ye'll be your pint-stowp!
And surely I'll be mine!
And we'll tak a cup o' kindness yet,
For auld lang syne.

CHORUS

We two hae run about the braes,
And pou'd the gowans fine;
But we've wander'd mony a weary foot
Sin auld lang syne

CHORUS

We two hae paidl'd i' the burn,
Frae morning sun till dine;
But sea between us braid hae roar'd
Sin auld lang syne.

CHORUS

And there's a hand my trusty fiere!
And gie's a hand o' thine!
And we'll tak a right gud-willy waught,
For auld lang syne.

CHORUS

The last line of the first verse and the chorus in this Scots version are now usually sung as 'For the sake of auld lang syne'. The English translation below is not normally sung but is instead a guide to understanding the Scots language.

ENGLISH TRANSLATION

Should old acquaintance be forgot,
And never brought to mind?
Should old acquaintance be forgot,
And times gone by?

CHORUS:

For days of long ago, my dear,
For days of long ago,
We'll take a cup of kindness yet,
For the sake of times gone by.

And surely you'll buy your pint cup!
And surely I'll buy mine!
And we'll take a cup of kindness yet,
For the sake of times gone by.

CHORUS

We two have run about the slopes,
And picked the daisies fine;
But we've wandered many a weary foot,
Since times gone by.

CHORUS

We two have paddled in the stream,
From morning sun till dine;
But seas between us broad have roared
Since times gone by.

CHORUS

And there's a hand my trusty friend!
And give me a hand of thine!

> And we'll take a right good-will draught,
> For the sake of times gone by.

CHORUS

Robert Burns wrote the words in 1788 but described it as a song of 'olden times', which he had never seen written down. The title and some of the lines are similar to 'Old Lang Syne', which had been published by James Watson in 1711, but Burns seems to have composed the rest. The custom of singing it on New Year's Eve quickly caught on in Scotland followed by the rest of Britain and many other parts of the world. The tune is probably an older Scottish air and 'syne' is an ancient Scottish word meaning 'old kindness'.

Bibliography

Cole, William, *Folk Songs of England, Ireland, Scotland & Wales*, Alfred Music, 1992.

Harrowven, Jean, *Origins of Rhymes, Songs and Sayings*, Pryor Publications, 1998.

Kennedy, Peter, ed., *Folksongs of Britain and Ireland*, Cassell, 1975.

Lomax, Alan, *The Penguin Book of American Folk Songs*, Penguin, 1964.

Roud, Steve, and Julia Bishop, *The New Penguin Book of English Folk Songs*, Penguin Classics, 2012.

Vaughan Williams, Ralph, *English Folk-Songs*, The English Folk Dance Society.

www.acousticmusicarchive.com
www.alangeorge.co.uk
www.azlyrics.com
www.carols.org.uk
www.classiccat.net
www.comebackhorslips.com
www.contemplator.com
www.folkstream.com
www.headington.org.uk
www.hymnary.org
www.ingeb.org
www.ireland-information.com
www.katerusby.com
www.lyricsmania.com
www.mainlynorfolk.info

www.metrolyrics.com
www.mudcat.org
www.musicanet.org
www.rampantscotland.com
www.royal.gov.uk
www.shanty.org.uk
www.thebards.net
www.traditionalmusic.co.uk
en.wikipedia.org
www.whychristmas.com
www.woodyguthrie.de
www.worldmusic.about.com
wordlymind.blogspot.co.uk
www.youtube.com

Picture Credits

Index of First Lines & Well-known Lines

First lines are in roman type and familiar or well-known lines are in italic type following a head word in bold italics.

**Also available from
Michael O'Mara Books**

Oranges and Lemons: Rhymes from Past Times
Karen Dolby ◆ 978-1-78243-485-6
£7.99 in paperback format ◆ Also in ebook